TEACHER'S PET PUBLICATIONS

PUZZLE PACK
for
The Crucible
based on the book by
Arthur Miller

Written by
William T. Collins

© 2005 Teacher's Pet Publications
All Rights Reserved

The materials in this packet are copyrighted
by Teacher's Pet Publications, Inc.

These pages may be duplicated by the purchaser
for use in the purchaser's own classroom.

Copying any of these materials and distributing them
for any other purpose is a violation of the copyright laws.

© 2005 Teacher's Pet Publications, Inc.
www.tpet.com

INTRODUCTION
If you already own the LitPlan for this title, this Puzzle Pack will refresh your Unit Resource Materials and Vocabulary Resource Materials sections plus give you additional materials you can substitute into the tests. If you do not already have a complete LitPlan, these pages will give you some supplemental materials to use with your own plan. There are two main groups of materials: one set for unit words (such as characters' names, symbols, places, etc.) and one set for vocabulary words associated with the book.

WORD LIST
There is a word list for both the unit words and the vocabulary words. These lists show you which words are being used in the materials and the clues or definitions being used for those words. You may want to give students a word list with clues/definitions to help them, or you may want students to only have a word list (without clues/definitions) if you want them to work a little harder. Both are available for duplication. The word lists can also be your "calling key" for the bingo games.

FILL IN THE BLANK AND MATCHING
There are 4 each of the fill in the blank and matching worksheets for both the unit and vocabulary words. These pages can be used either as extra worksheets for students or as objective parts of a unit test. They can be done individually if students need extra help or as a whole class activity to review the material covered.

MAGIC SQUARES
The magic squares not only reinforce the material covered but also work on reasoning and math skills. Many teachers have told us that their students really enjoy doing these!

WORD SEARCH PUZZLES
The word search words go in all directions, as indicated on your answer keys. Two of the word search puzzles have the clues listed rather than the words. This makes the puzzle a little more difficult, but it reinforces the material better. Two word search puzzles have words only for students who find the clue puzzles too difficult.

CROSSWORD PUZZLES
Both unit and vocabulary word sections have 4 crossword puzzles.

BINGO CARDS
There are 32 individual bingo cards for the unit words and 32 individual bingo cards for the vocabulary words. You can use your word list as a "call list," calling the words at random and marking them off of your list as you go, or you could use the flash cards by cutting them apart and drawing the words at random from a hat (or box or whatever). To make a better review, you might ask for the definition and spelling of each word as you call it out–or you could call out the definitions and have students tell you the words they need to look for on the puzzle.

JUGGLE LETTERS
The vocabulary juggle letter game is intended to help students learn the spellings of the words. One sheet has the definitions listed on it as an extra help for students who need it or to reinforce the definitions if you choose to do so.

FLASH CARDS
We've included a set of vocabulary flash cards you can duplicate, cut, and fold for your students. Some teachers make a few sets for general use by the class; others make a set for each student. Some teachers duplicate them for each student and have the students cut & fold their own. You can cut out just the words and put them in a hat, have each student pick out one word and write the definition and a sentence for that word. Students then swap words and papers, with the next student adding a sentence of his own under the last one. You can have students swap as many times as you like. Each time the student will read the sentences written prior to his own and then add a sentence. You can cut out the words and definitions separately and play "I Have; Who Has?" Each student in the room draws a word and definition. The first student says, "I have (the name of the word). Who has the definition?" The student with the definition reads it then says, "I have (the name of the vocabulary word she has). Who has the definition?" The round continues until all words and definitions have been given.

The Crucible Unit Word List

No.	Word	Clue/Definition
1.	ABIGAIL	She is the primary cause of the witch hunts
2.	ACT	Play division
3.	ADULTERY	The commandment Proctor forgets
4.	BABIES	Many of Mrs. Putnam's have died
5.	BETTY	Parris' daughter
6.	BIBLE	The christian holy book
7.	BITTER	Thomas Putnam was this about his situation in life
8.	BOOKS	Reading material
9.	CHEEVER	He arrests Elizabeth
10.	CHURCH	God's house
11.	COMMANDMENTS	Moses gave christians 10 of these
12.	CONFESSION	Admission
13.	COREY	Giles
14.	DANCE	Move with rhythm
15.	DANFORTH	The judge for many witchcraft trials
16.	DEVIL	Satan
17.	ELIZABETH	John's wife
18.	EVIDENCE	Material proof
19.	EVIL	Bad
20.	FIREWOOD	Parris wanted a deed and this along with his salary
21.	FOREST	Meeting place of Tituba and the devil
22.	FRANCIS	Mr. Nurse
23.	GILES	Mr. Corey
24.	GOD	The Creator
25.	GOOD	Opposite of bad
26.	GOODNESS	Rebecca is full of it
27.	GUILT	Conscience's nagging feeling
28.	HALE	He was an expert spirit remover
29.	HANG	Method of execution using a rope
30.	HAWTHORNE	He thinks of a test for Mary
31.	HONEST	One who tells the truth is this
32.	INDIVIDUAL	Alone; not as a member of a group
33.	JUDGE	Decision maker in court
34.	LAND	Object of the Putnams' dispute with the Nurses
35.	MARY	She wants Abby to tell the truth
36.	NURSE	Rebecca
37.	PARRIS	Betty's father and Abigail's uncle
38.	PLAY	Story written to be performed on the stage
39.	POPPET	Gift from Mary to Elizabeth
40.	PRETENSE	The act of pretending
41.	PROCTOR	John; he tries to make people see the truth
42.	PUTNAM	Ann or Thomas
43.	REBECCA	Mrs. Nurse
44.	SCENE	Division of an act
45.	SIGN	Something that shows the existence of a fact
46.	SOUL	If Proctor tells the truth, he will save his
47.	SPIRITS	Ghosts, beings
48.	TITUBA	Parris' slave woman from Barbados
49.	TRIAL	Examination of evidence to determine guilt or innocence
50.	WITCH	Woman who pracitces witchcraft
51.	WITCHCRAFT	Black magic; sorcery
52.	WORSHIP	To adore

The Crucible Fil In The Blank 1

_____ 1. The judge for many witchcraft trials

_____ 2. Betty's father and Abigail's uncle

_____ 3. If Proctor tells the truth, he will save his

_____ 4. Examination of evidence to determine guilt or innocence

_____ 5. Decision maker in court

_____ 6. John; he tries to make people see the truth

_____ 7. Material proof

_____ 8. He thinks of a test for Mary

_____ 9. Alone; not as a member of a group

_____ 10. The Creator

_____ 11. Giles

_____ 12. Parris' slave woman from Barbados

_____ 13. Play division

_____ 14. One who tells the truth is this

_____ 15. He arrests Elizabeth

_____ 16. Black magic; sorcery

_____ 17. John's wife

_____ 18. The commandment Proctor forgets

_____ 19. Division of an act

_____ 20. Story written to be performed on the stage

The Crucible Fill In The Blank 1 Answer Key

DANFORTH	1.	The judge for many witchcraft trials
PARRIS	2.	Betty's father and Abigail's uncle
SOUL	3.	If Proctor tells the truth, he will save his
TRIAL	4.	Examination of evidence to determine guilt or innocence
JUDGE	5.	Decision maker in court
PROCTOR	6.	John; he tries to make people see the truth
EVIDENCE	7.	Material proof
HAWTHORNE	8.	He thinks of a test for Mary
INDIVIDUAL	9.	Alone; not as a member of a group
GOD	10.	The Creator
COREY	11.	Giles
TITUBA	12.	Parris' slave woman from Barbados
ACT	13.	Play division
HONEST	14.	One who tells the truth is this
CHEEVER	15.	He arrests Elizabeth
WITCHCRAFT	16.	Black magic; sorcery
ELIZABETH	17.	John's wife
ADULTERY	18.	The commandment Proctor forgets
SCENE	19.	Division of an act
PLAY	20.	Story written to be performed on the stage

The Crucible Fill In The Blank 2

1. Division of an act
2. Rebecca is full of it
3. Move with rhythm
4. Moses gave christians 10 of these
5. Reading material
6. Material proof
7. He was an expert spirit remover
8. The judge for many witchcraft trials
9. Woman who pracitces witchcraft
10. If Proctor tells the truth, he will save his
11. Conscience's nagging feeling
12. The commandment Proctor forgets
13. Story written to be performed on the stage
14. Play division
15. Many of Mrs. Putnam's have died
16. The act of pretending
17. Giles
18. Admission
19. He arrests Elizabeth
20. The Creator

The Crucible Fill In The Blank 2 Answer Key

Answer	Clue
SCENE	1. Division of an act
GOODNESS	2. Rebecca is full of it
DANCE	3. Move with rhythm
COMMANDMENTS	4. Moses gave christians 10 of these
BOOKS	5. Reading material
EVIDENCE	6. Material proof
HALE	7. He was an expert spirit remover
DANFORTH	8. The judge for many witchcraft trials
WITCH	9. Woman who pracitces witchcraft
SOUL	10. If Proctor tells the truth, he will save his
GUILT	11. Conscience's nagging feeling
ADULTERY	12. The commandment Proctor forgets
PLAY	13. Story written to be performed on the stage
ACT	14. Play division
BABIES	15. Many of Mrs. Putnam's have died
PRETENSE	16. The act of pretending
COREY	17. Giles
CONFESSION	18. Admission
CHEEVER	19. He arrests Elizabeth
GOD	20. The Creator

The Crucible Fill In The Blank 3

_____ 1. The christian holy book

_____ 2. Parris wanted a deed and this along with his salary

_____ 3. She is the primary cause of the witch hunts

_____ 4. Decision maker in court

_____ 5. Mr. Nurse

_____ 6. Satan

_____ 7. Gift from Mary to Elizabeth

_____ 8. Conscience's nagging feeling

_____ 9. Something that shows the existence of a fact

_____ 10. God's house

_____ 11. Many of Mrs. Putnam's have died

_____ 12. To adore

_____ 13. Parris' slave woman from Barbados

_____ 14. Method of execution using a rope

_____ 15. Thomas Putnam was this about his situation in life

_____ 16. Bad

_____ 17. He thinks of a test for Mary

_____ 18. Ann or Thomas

_____ 19. Black magic; sorcery

_____ 20. John's wife

The Crucible Fill In The Blank 3 Answer Key

BIBLE	1. The christian holy book
FIREWOOD	2. Parris wanted a deed and this along with his salary
ABIGAIL	3. She is the primary cause of the witch hunts
JUDGE	4. Decision maker in court
FRANCIS	5. Mr. Nurse
DEVIL	6. Satan
POPPET	7. Gift from Mary to Elizabeth
GUILT	8. Conscience's nagging feeling
SIGN	9. Something that shows the existence of a fact
CHURCH	10. God's house
BABIES	11. Many of Mrs. Putnam's have died
WORSHIP	12. To adore
TITUBA	13. Parris' slave woman from Barbados
HANG	14. Method of execution using a rope
BITTER	15. Thomas Putnam was this about his situation in life
EVIL	16. Bad
HAWTHORNE	17. He thinks of a test for Mary
PUTNAM	18. Ann or Thomas
WITCHCRAFT	19. Black magic; sorcery
ELIZABETH	20. John's wife

The Crucible Fill In The Blank 4

_____ 1. The judge for many witchcraft trials

_____ 2. Parris' daughter

_____ 3. Play division

_____ 4. Thomas Putnam was this about his situation in life

_____ 5. Conscience's nagging feeling

_____ 6. Rebecca

_____ 7. Division of an act

_____ 8. She is the primary cause of the witch hunts

_____ 9. The Creator

_____ 10. Gift from Mary to Elizabeth

_____ 11. The commandment Proctor forgets

_____ 12. The act of pretending

_____ 13. Something that shows the existence of a fact

_____ 14. Story written to be performed on the stage

_____ 15. Ghosts, beings

_____ 16. Betty's father and Abigail's uncle

_____ 17. Material proof

_____ 18. John's wife

_____ 19. Mrs. Nurse

_____ 20. Meeting place of Tituba and the devil

The Crucible Fill In The Blank 4 Answer Key

DANFORTH	1. The judge for many witchcraft trials
BETTY	2. Parris' daughter
ACT	3. Play division
BITTER	4. Thomas Putnam was this about his situation in life
GUILT	5. Conscience's nagging feeling
NURSE	6. Rebecca
SCENE	7. Division of an act
ABIGAIL	8. She is the primary cause of the witch hunts
GOD	9. The Creator
POPPET	10. Gift from Mary to Elizabeth
ADULTERY	11. The commandment Proctor forgets
PRETENSE	12. The act of pretending
SIGN	13. Something that shows the existence of a fact
PLAY	14. Story written to be performed on the stage
SPIRITS	15. Ghosts, beings
PARRIS	16. Betty's father and Abigail's uncle
EVIDENCE	17. Material proof
ELIZABETH	18. John's wife
REBECCA	19. Mrs. Nurse
FOREST	20. Meeting place of Tituba and the devil

Copyrighted

The Crucible Matching 1

___ 1. PARRIS   A. One who tells the truth is this
___ 2. HONEST   B. The judge for many witchcraft trials
___ 3. EVIL   C. Meeting place of Tituba and the devil
___ 4. WITCHCRAFT   D. Conscience's nagging feeling
___ 5. COREY   E. Ghosts, beings
___ 6. GUILT   F. Rebecca
___ 7. ADULTERY   G. Admission
___ 8. SPIRITS   H. Many of Mrs. Putnam's have died
___ 9. REBECCA   I. Opposite of bad
___10. SCENE   J. The commandment Proctor forgets
___11. INDIVIDUAL   K. Ann or Thomas
___12. WITCH   L. Division of an act
___13. PLAY   M. Reading material
___14. DANFORTH   N. Rebecca is full of it
___15. BOOKS   O. Giles
___16. HAWTHORNE   P. Mrs. Nurse
___17. BABIES   Q. He thinks of a test for Mary
___18. CONFESSION   R. Story written to be performed on the stage
___19. GILES   S. Mr. Corey
___20. CHURCH   T. Woman who pracitces witchcraft
___21. PUTNAM   U. Bad
___22. FOREST   V. Alone; not as a member of a group
___23. NURSE   W. Black magic; sorcery
___24. GOOD   X. Betty's father and Abigail's uncle
___25. GOODNESS   Y. God's house

The Crucible Matching 1 Answer Key

X - 1. PARRIS	A.	One who tells the truth is this
A - 2. HONEST	B.	The judge for many witchcraft trials
U - 3. EVIL	C.	Meeting place of Tituba and the devil
W - 4. WITCHCRAFT	D.	Conscience's nagging feeling
O - 5. COREY	E.	Ghosts, beings
D - 6. GUILT	F.	Rebecca
J - 7. ADULTERY	G.	Admission
E - 8. SPIRITS	H.	Many of Mrs. Putnam's have died
P - 9. REBECCA	I.	Opposite of bad
L - 10. SCENE	J.	The commandment Proctor forgets
V - 11. INDIVIDUAL	K.	Ann or Thomas
T - 12. WITCH	L.	Division of an act
R - 13. PLAY	M.	Reading material
B - 14. DANFORTH	N.	Rebecca is full of it
M - 15. BOOKS	O.	Giles
Q - 16. HAWTHORNE	P.	Mrs. Nurse
H - 17. BABIES	Q.	He thinks of a test for Mary
G - 18. CONFESSION	R.	Story written to be performed on the stage
S - 19. GILES	S.	Mr. Corey
Y - 20. CHURCH	T.	Woman who pracitces witchcraft
K - 21. PUTNAM	U.	Bad
C - 22. FOREST	V.	Alone; not as a member of a group
F - 23. NURSE	W.	Black magic; sorcery
I - 24. GOOD	X.	Betty's father and Abigail's uncle
N - 25. GOODNESS	Y.	God's house

The Crucible Matching 2

___ 1. FIREWOOD   A. Ann or Thomas
___ 2. DEVIL   B. The act of pretending
___ 3. SOUL   C. Parris wanted a deed and this along with his salary
___ 4. BABIES   D. Moses gave christians 10 of these
___ 5. WITCHCRAFT   E. Many of Mrs. Putnam's have died
___ 6. GOOD   F. If Proctor tells the truth, he will save his
___ 7. ELIZABETH   G. Satan
___ 8. COREY   H. Story written to be performed on the stage
___ 9. POPPET   I. Examination of evidence to determine guilt or innocence
___ 10. TRIAL   J. Giles
___ 11. PUTNAM   K. Something that shows the existence of a fact
___ 12. COMMANDMENTS   L. He thinks of a test for Mary
___ 13. NURSE   M. He arrests Elizabeth
___ 14. LAND   N. Conscience's nagging feeling
___ 15. SIGN   O. To adore
___ 16. PRETENSE   P. He was an expert spirit remover
___ 17. PLAY   Q. Object of the Putnams' dispute with the Nurses
___ 18. GUILT   R. Gift from Mary to Elizabeth
___ 19. GOODNESS   S. Rebecca is full of it
___ 20. WORSHIP   T. The judge for many witchcraft trials
___ 21. HAWTHORNE   U. John's wife
___ 22. CHEEVER   V. Opposite of bad
___ 23. HALE   W. Mrs. Nurse
___ 24. REBECCA   X. Rebecca
___ 25. DANFORTH   Y. Black magic; sorcery

The Crucible Matching 2 Answer Key

C - 1. FIREWOOD	A. Ann or Thomas
G - 2. DEVIL	B. The act of pretending
F - 3. SOUL	C. Parris wanted a deed and this along with his salary
E - 4. BABIES	D. Moses gave christians 10 of these
Y - 5. WITCHCRAFT	E. Many of Mrs. Putnam's have died
V - 6. GOOD	F. If Proctor tells the truth, he will save his
U - 7. ELIZABETH	G. Satan
J - 8. COREY	H. Story written to be performed on the stage
R - 9. POPPET	I. Examination of evidence to determine guilt or innocence
I - 10. TRIAL	J. Giles
A - 11. PUTNAM	K. Something that shows the existence of a fact
D - 12. COMMANDMENTS	L. He thinks of a test for Mary
X - 13. NURSE	M. He arrests Elizabeth
Q - 14. LAND	N. Conscience's nagging feeling
K - 15. SIGN	O. To adore
B - 16. PRETENSE	P. He was an expert spirit remover
H - 17. PLAY	Q. Object of the Putnams' dispute with the Nurses
N - 18. GUILT	R. Gift from Mary to Elizabeth
S - 19. GOODNESS	S. Rebecca is full of it
O - 20. WORSHIP	T. The judge for many witchcraft trials
L - 21. HAWTHORNE	U. John's wife
M - 22. CHEEVER	V. Opposite of bad
P - 23. HALE	W. Mrs. Nurse
W - 24. REBECCA	X. Rebecca
T - 25. DANFORTH	Y. Black magic; sorcery

The Crucible Matching 3

___ 1. HALE
___ 2. ACT
___ 3. REBECCA
___ 4. PLAY
___ 5. GOODNESS
___ 6. POPPET
___ 7. SOUL
___ 8. ADULTERY
___ 9. ELIZABETH
___10. BOOKS
___11. HONEST
___12. PUTNAM
___13. MARY
___14. GILES
___15. WITCHCRAFT
___16. INDIVIDUAL
___17. CHURCH
___18. TRIAL
___19. GOD
___20. CHEEVER
___21. CONFESSION
___22. PARRIS
___23. WITCH
___24. SCENE
___25. PROCTOR

A. She wants Abby to tell the truth
B. Mr. Corey
C. Mrs. Nurse
D. Division of an act
E. Admission
F. Examination of evidence to determine guilt or innocence
G. If Proctor tells the truth, he will save his
H. Betty's father and Abigail's uncle
I. Reading material
J. John's wife
K. He arrests Elizabeth
L. Alone; not as a member of a group
M. God's house
N. The commandment Proctor forgets
O. Woman who pracitces witchcraft
P. John; he tries to make people see the truth
Q. One who tells the truth is this
R. Black magic; sorcery
S. Rebecca is full of it
T. He was an expert spirit remover
U. The Creator
V. Play division
W. Ann or Thomas
X. Story written to be performed on the stage
Y. Gift from Mary to Elizabeth

The Crucible Matching 3 Answer Key

T - 1. HALE A. She wants Abby to tell the truth
V - 2. ACT B. Mr. Corey
C - 3. REBECCA C. Mrs. Nurse
X - 4. PLAY D. Division of an act
S - 5. GOODNESS E. Admission
Y - 6. POPPET F. Examination of evidence to determine guilt or innocence
G - 7. SOUL G. If Proctor tells the truth, he will save his
N - 8. ADULTERY H. Betty's father and Abigail's uncle
J - 9. ELIZABETH I. Reading material
I - 10. BOOKS J. John's wife
Q -11. HONEST K. He arrests Elizabeth
W -12. PUTNAM L. Alone; not as a member of a group
A -13. MARY M. God's house
B -14. GILES N. The commandment Proctor forgets
R -15. WITCHCRAFT O. Woman who pracitces witchcraft
L -16. INDIVIDUAL P. John; he tries to make people see the truth
M -17. CHURCH Q. One who tells the truth is this
F -18. TRIAL R. Black magic; sorcery
U -19. GOD S. Rebecca is full of it
K -20. CHEEVER T. He was an expert spirit remover
E -21. CONFESSION U. The Creator
H -22. PARRIS V. Play division
O -23. WITCH W. Ann or Thomas
D -24. SCENE X. Story written to be performed on the stage
P -25. PROCTOR Y. Gift from Mary to Elizabeth

The Crucible Matching 4

___ 1. HONEST
___ 2. WITCHCRAFT
___ 3. BABIES
___ 4. LAND
___ 5. SOUL
___ 6. GOOD
___ 7. FOREST
___ 8. DANCE
___ 9. DANFORTH
___ 10. TITUBA
___ 11. HANG
___ 12. MARY
___ 13. WORSHIP
___ 14. PUTNAM
___ 15. BIBLE
___ 16. FRANCIS
___ 17. BITTER
___ 18. ELIZABETH
___ 19. INDIVIDUAL
___ 20. BOOKS
___ 21. GOD
___ 22. WITCH
___ 23. PLAY
___ 24. ABIGAIL
___ 25. HAWTHORNE

A. Parris' slave woman from Barbados
B. Object of the Putnams' dispute with the Nurses
C. Meeting place of Tituba and the devil
D. If Proctor tells the truth, he will save his
E. Method of execution using a rope
F. He thinks of a test for Mary
G. Story written to be performed on the stage
H. Black magic; sorcery
I. Woman who pracitces witchcraft
J. Opposite of bad
K. She wants Abby to tell the truth
L. Mr. Nurse
M. The christian holy book
N. Thomas Putnam was this about his situation in life
O. Alone; not as a member of a group
P. The judge for many witchcraft trials
Q. Many of Mrs. Putnam's have died
R. Reading material
S. Ann or Thomas
T. The Creator
U. To adore
V. Move with rhythm
W. She is the primary cause of the witch hunts
X. One who tells the truth is this
Y. John's wife

The Crucible Matching 4 Answer Key

X - 1.	HONEST	A. Parris' slave woman from Barbados
H - 2.	WITCHCRAFT	B. Object of the Putnams' dispute with the Nurses
Q - 3.	BABIES	C. Meeting place of Tituba and the devil
B - 4.	LAND	D. If Proctor tells the truth, he will save his
D - 5.	SOUL	E. Method of execution using a rope
J - 6.	GOOD	F. He thinks of a test for Mary
C - 7.	FOREST	G. Story written to be performed on the stage
V - 8.	DANCE	H. Black magic; sorcery
P - 9.	DANFORTH	I. Woman who pracitces witchcraft
A - 10.	TITUBA	J. Opposite of bad
E - 11.	HANG	K. She wants Abby to tell the truth
K - 12.	MARY	L. Mr. Nurse
U - 13.	WORSHIP	M. The christian holy book
S - 14.	PUTNAM	N. Thomas Putnam was this about his situation in life
M - 15.	BIBLE	O. Alone; not as a member of a group
L - 16.	FRANCIS	P. The judge for many witchcraft trials
N - 17.	BITTER	Q. Many of Mrs. Putnam's have died
Y - 18.	ELIZABETH	R. Reading material
O - 19.	INDIVIDUAL	S. Ann or Thomas
R - 20.	BOOKS	T. The Creator
T - 21.	GOD	U. To adore
I - 22.	WITCH	V. Move with rhythm
G - 23.	PLAY	W. She is the primary cause of the witch hunts
W - 24.	ABIGAIL	X. One who tells the truth is this
F - 25.	HAWTHORNE	Y. John's wife

Copyrighted

The Crucible Magic Squares 1

Match the definition with the vocabulary word. Put your answers in the magic squares below. When your answers are correct, all columns and rows will add to the same number.

A. EVIL
B. BIBLE
C. REBECCA
D. LAND
E. WORSHIP
F. ACT
G. GOODNESS
H. BETTY
I. GILES
J. SPIRITS
K. INDIVIDUAL
L. FIREWOOD
M. ADULTERY
N. JUDGE
O. SIGN
P. BABIES

1. Something that shows the existence of a fact
2. Object of the Putnams' dispute with the Nurses
3. Ghosts, beings
4. To adore
5. Mr. Corey
6. Play division
7. Many of Mrs. Putnam's have died
8. Mrs. Nurse
9. Parris' daughter
10. Alone; not as a member of a group
11. Bad
12. Decision maker in court
13. The christian holy book
14. The commandment Proctor forgets
15. Rebecca is full of it
16. Parris wanted a deed and this along with his salary

A=	B=	C=	D=
E=	F=	G=	H=
I=	J=	K=	L=
M=	N=	O=	P=

The Crucible Magic Squares 1 Answer Key

Match the definition with the vocabulary word. Put your answers in the magic squares below. When your answers are correct, all columns and rows will add to the same number.

A. EVIL
B. BIBLE
C. REBECCA
D. LAND
E. WORSHIP
F. ACT
G. GOODNESS
H. BETTY
I. GILES
J. SPIRITS
K. INDIVIDUAL
L. FIREWOOD
M. ADULTERY
N. JUDGE
O. SIGN
P. BABIES

1. Something that shows the existence of a fact
2. Object of the Putnams' dispute with the Nurses
3. Ghosts, beings
4. To adore
5. Mr. Corey
6. Play division
7. Many of Mrs. Putnam's have died
8. Mrs. Nurse
9. Parris' daughter
10. Alone; not as a member of a group
11. Bad
12. Decision maker in court
13. The christian holy book
14. The commandment Proctor forgets
15. Rebecca is full of it
16. Parris wanted a deed and this along with his salary

A=11	B=13	C=8	D=2
E=4	F=6	G=15	H=9
I=5	J=3	K=10	L=16
M=14	N=12	O=1	P=7

The Crucible Magic Squares 2

Match the definition with the vocabulary word. Put your answers in the magic squares below. When your answers are correct, all columns and rows will add to the same number.

A. EVIL
B. POPPET
C. SCENE
D. CHEEVER
E. PARRIS
F. SIGN
G. WITCH
H. HAWTHORNE
I. FIREWOOD
J. PRETENSE
K. GOODNESS
L. BOOKS
M. GILES
N. PUTNAM
O. HONEST
P. JUDGE

1. Mr. Corey
2. Something that shows the existence of a fact
3. He thinks of a test for Mary
4. One who tells the truth is this
5. Reading material
6. Division of an act
7. Bad
8. The act of pretending
9. Rebecca is full of it
10. He arrests Elizabeth
11. Gift from Mary to Elizabeth
12. Parris wanted a deed and this along with his salary
13. Ann or Thomas
14. Betty's father and Abigail's uncle
15. Woman who pracitces witchcraft
16. Decision maker in court

A=	B=	C=	D=
E=	F=	G=	H=
I=	J=	K=	L=
M=	N=	O=	P=

The Crucible Magic Squares 2 Answer Key

Match the definition with the vocabulary word. Put your answers in the magic squares below. When your answers are correct, all columns and rows will add to the same number.

A. EVIL
B. POPPET
C. SCENE
D. CHEEVER
E. PARRIS
F. SIGN
G. WITCH
H. HAWTHORNE
I. FIREWOOD
J. PRETENSE
K. GOODNESS
L. BOOKS
M. GILES
N. PUTNAM
O. HONEST
P. JUDGE

1. Mr. Corey
2. Something that shows the existence of a fact
3. He thinks of a test for Mary
4. One who tells the truth is this
5. Reading material
6. Division of an act
7. Bad
8. The act of pretending
9. Rebecca is full of it
10. He arrests Elizabeth
11. Gift from Mary to Elizabeth
12. Parris wanted a deed and this along with his salary
13. Ann or Thomas
14. Betty's father and Abigail's uncle
15. Woman who pracitces witchcraft
16. Decision maker in court

A=7	B=11	C=6	D=10
E=14	F=2	G=15	H=3
I=12	J=8	K=9	L=5
M=1	N=13	O=4	P=16

The Crucible Magic Squares 3

Match the definition with the vocabulary word. Put your answers in the magic squares below. When your answers are correct, all columns and rows will add to the same number.

A. ADULTERY
B. WORSHIP
C. DANCE
D. GUILT
E. REBECCA
F. HALE
G. BITTER
H. HANG
I. PLAY
J. HAWTHORNE
K. LAND
L. COREY
M. GOODNESS
N. FOREST
O. BIBLE
P. CONFESSION

1. Move with rhythm
2. He thinks of a test for Mary
3. He was an expert spirit remover
4. The christian holy book
5. Admission
6. Mrs. Nurse
7. Story written to be performed on the stage
8. Conscience's nagging feeling
9. Rebecca is full of it
10. Method of execution using a rope
11. Giles
12. The commandment Proctor forgets
13. To adore
14. Object of the Putnams' dispute with the Nurses
15. Thomas Putnam was this about his situation in life
16. Meeting place of Tituba and the devil

A=	B=	C=	D=
E=	F=	G=	H=
I=	J=	K=	L=
M=	N=	O=	P=

The Crucible Magic Squares 3 Answer Key

Match the definition with the vocabulary word. Put your answers in the magic squares below. When your answers are correct, all columns and rows will add to the same number.

A. ADULTERY
B. WORSHIP
C. DANCE
D. GUILT
E. REBECCA
F. HALE
G. BITTER
H. HANG
I. PLAY
J. HAWTHORNE
K. LAND
L. COREY
M. GOODNESS
N. FOREST
O. BIBLE
P. CONFESSION

1. Move with rhythm
2. He thinks of a test for Mary
3. He was an expert spirit remover
4. The christian holy book
5. Admission
6. Mrs. Nurse
7. Story written to be performed on the stage
8. Conscience's nagging feeling
9. Rebecca is full of it
10. Method of execution using a rope
11. Giles
12. The commandment Proctor forgets
13. To adore
14. Object of the Putnams' dispute with the Nurses
15. Thomas Putnam was this about his situation in life
16. Meeting place of Tituba and the devil

A=12	B=13	C=1	D=8
E=6	F=3	G=15	H=10
I=7	J=2	K=14	L=11
M=9	N=16	O=4	P=5

The Crucible Magic Squares 4

Match the definition with the vocabulary word. Put your answers in the magic squares below. When your answers are correct, all columns and rows will add to the same number.

A. ABIGAIL
B. BETTY
C. CHURCH
D. FRANCIS
E. BOOKS
F. FOREST
G. PROCTOR
H. BITTER
I. GOD
J. NURSE
K. GOOD
L. BIBLE
M. DANCE
N. GILES
O. ELIZABETH
P. SPIRITS

1. John's wife
2. Rebecca
3. Thomas Putnam was this about his situation in life
4. She is the primary cause of the witch hunts
5. Mr. Nurse
6. Reading material
7. Opposite of bad
8. Mr. Corey
9. Meeting place of Tituba and the devil
10. God's house
11. Move with rhythm
12. The christian holy book
13. The Creator
14. Ghosts, beings
15. Parris' daughter
16. John; he tries to make people see the truth

A=	B=	C=	D=
E=	F=	G=	H=
I=	J=	K=	L=
M=	N=	O=	P=

The Crucible Magic Squares 4 Answer Key

Match the definition with the vocabulary word. Put your answers in the magic squares below. When your answers are correct, all columns and rows will add to the same number.

A. ABIGAIL
B. BETTY
C. CHURCH
D. FRANCIS
E. BOOKS
F. FOREST
G. PROCTOR
H. BITTER
I. GOD
J. NURSE
K. GOOD
L. BIBLE
M. DANCE
N. GILES
O. ELIZABETH
P. SPIRITS

1. John's wife
2. Rebecca
3. Thomas Putnam was this about his situation in life
4. She is the primary cause of the witch hunts
5. Mr. Nurse
6. Reading material
7. Opposite of bad
8. Mr. Corey
9. Meeting place of Tituba and the devil
10. God's house
11. Move with rhythm
12. The christian holy book
13. The Creator
14. Ghosts, beings
15. Parris' daughter
16. John; he tries to make people see the truth

A=4	B=15	C=10	D=5
E=6	F=9	G=16	H=3
I=13	J=2	K=7	L=12
M=11	N=8	O=1	P=14

The Crucible Word Search 1

```
B I T T E R C W L T H W P H J Y G D H W
R J G P F G H T O W N I B Y R E U R A L
E T Z R R S E Q E R F T Q A G R I Y W T
B I S O A L E L V F S C M X L O L K T Z
E T C C N C V S I H I H P H A C T P H C
C U E T C O E J L Z N R I A I M R V O W
C B N O I M R V W J A Y E P R E G G R F
A A E R S M P L A Y T B W W T R H Z N R
C B K F S A I T H T C L E E O T I N E M
P P A S W N R N E T R H N T R O J S V J
W O F B X D P B D L P S U O H T D W D D
R N P Z I M G G F I E B F R R M W T Z
N R F P M E K O S V V N J D C C D S T V
G X G S E N S X O E A I U Z A H E H F C
F O R E S T L A N D G O D M A N T U P J
B L J B I S B R W V N P G U O H C N Y Y
O V S R V V I J H J D E E H A S A E Q S
O G I L E S B A J O H T S A P L O N Y Y
K P G H K H L P O G K H W S C C P U G D
S D N Y N E E G N U R S E D V T G V L B
```

Alone; not as a member of a group (10)
Ann or Thomas (6)
Bad (4)
Betty's father and Abigail's uncle (6)
Conscience's nagging feeling (5)
Decision maker in court (5)
Division of an act (5)
Examination of evidence to determine guilt or innocence (5)
Ghosts, beings (7)
Gift from Mary to Elizabeth (6)
Giles (5)
God's house (6)
He arrests Elizabeth (7)
He thinks of a test for Mary (9)
He was an expert spirit remover (4)
If Proctor tells the truth, he will save his (4)
John's wife (9)
John; he tries to make people see the truth (7)
Many of Mrs. Putnam's have died (6)
Meeting place of Tituba and the devil (6)
Method of execution using a rope (4)
Moses gave christians 10 of these (12)
Move with rhythm (5)
Mr. Corey (5)
Mr. Nurse (7)
Mrs. Nurse (7)
Object of the Putnams' dispute with the Nurses (4)
One who tells the truth is this (6)
Opposite of bad (4)
Parris wanted a deed and this along with his salary (8)
Parris' daughter (5)
Parris' slave woman from Barbados (6)
Play division (3)
Reading material (5)
Rebecca (5)
Rebecca is full of it (8)
Satan (5)
She wants Abby to tell the truth (4)
Something that shows the existence of a fact (4)
Story written to be performed on the stage (4)
The Creator (3)
The act of pretending (8)
The christian holy book (5)
The judge for many witchcraft trials (8)
Thomas Putnam was this about his situation in life (6)
To adore (7)
Woman who pracitces witchcraft (5)

The Crucible Word Search 1 Answer Key

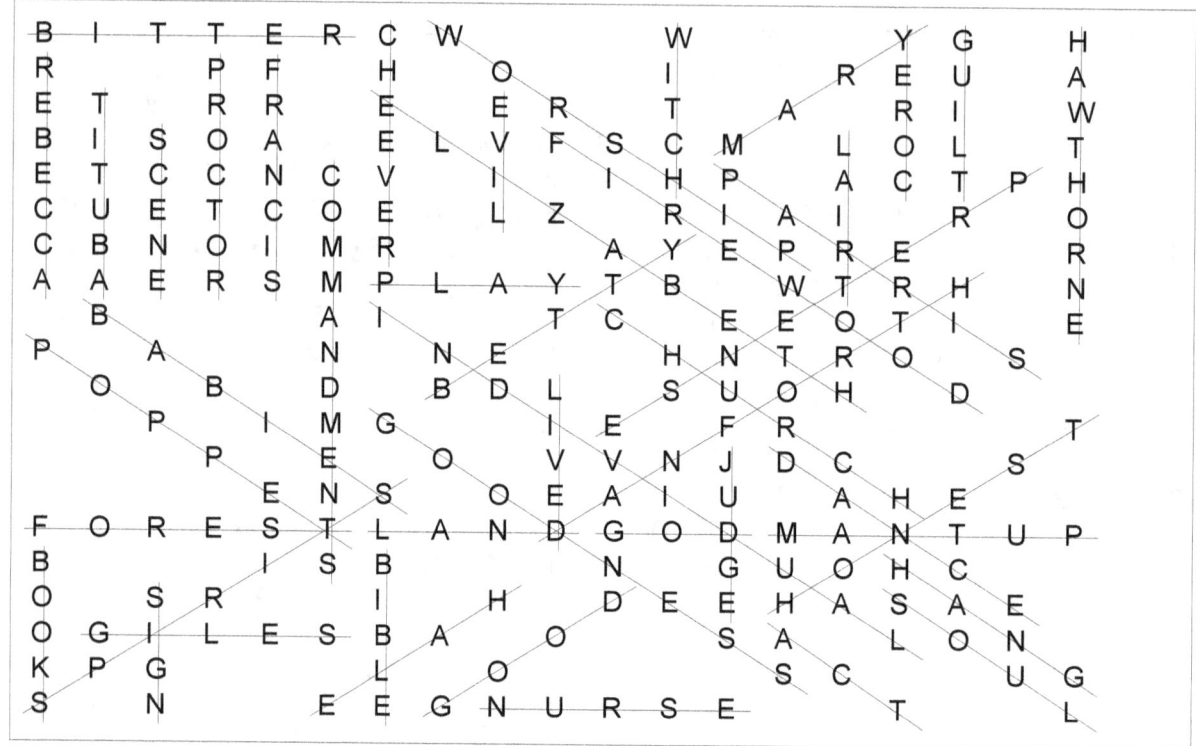

Alone; not as a member of a group (10)
Ann or Thomas (6)
Bad (4)
Betty's father and Abigail's uncle (6)
Conscience's nagging feeling (5)
Decision maker in court (5)
Division of an act (5)
Examination of evidence to determine guilt or innocence (5)
Ghosts, beings (7)
Gift from Mary to Elizabeth (6)
Giles (5)
God's house (6)
He arrests Elizabeth (7)
He thinks of a test for Mary (9)
He was an expert spirit remover (4)
If Proctor tells the truth, he will save his (4)
John's wife (9)
John; he tries to make people see the truth (7)
Many of Mrs. Putnam's have died (6)
Meeting place of Tituba and the devil (6)
Method of execution using a rope (4)
Moses gave christians 10 of these (12)
Move with rhythm (5)
Mr. Corey (5)
Mr. Nurse (7)
Mrs. Nurse (7)
Object of the Putnams' dispute with the Nurses (4)
One who tells the truth is this (6)
Opposite of bad (4)
Parris wanted a deed and this along with his salary (8)
Parris' daughter (5)
Parris' slave woman from Barbados (6)
Play division (3)
Reading material (5)
Rebecca (5)
Rebecca is full of it (8)
Satan (5)
She wants Abby to tell the truth (4)
Something that shows the existence of a fact (4)
Story written to be performed on the stage (4)
The Creator (3)
The act of pretending (8)
The christian holy book (5)
The judge for many witchcraft trials (8)
Thomas Putnam was this about his situation in life (6)
To adore (7)
Woman who pracitces witchcraft (5)

The Crucible Word Search 2

```
C X D E S N E T E R P S H A J U D G E R
M T H E B X B D C P T P X D N Q Q W C M
P B L P G I B A O X V I H U S F N F H C
W I S Y U F T P B V X R B L C R Z L U M
G I A M I B P T Y I R I E T E R I F R N
K L T S L E Y H E W E T T E N V N Q C K
P R O C T O R F O R E S T R E V E E H C
G R L O H D T R L N I V Y Y E C W A K H
O N W R X P S J M R E L I L C B N W H Q
O U D E L H C L R J J S A D F G E G B G
D R L Y I B Z A D M C I T N E P J C S G
N S Y P V P P K A O R J S L D N F I C F
E E C R E X K D N T R W I Q X D C Z L A
S Y B L D T M F C L P A G J O N D E Y R
S K A N C B E V E T G S N O A Y N D L J
F H S B L S S H Y I K E W R H C F L M P
Y X K C S F O S B V L E F P U T N A M K
T P O I F G U A K B R W C D B C R P T R
G O O D W O L Q I I V M Q G R Y Y C C G
F N B Q J D N B F T I T U B A N A L X F
```

Admission (10)
Ann or Thomas (6)
Bad (4)
Betty's father and Abigail's uncle (6)
Conscience's nagging feeling (5)
Decision maker in court (5)
Division of an act (5)
Examination of evidence to determine guilt or innocence (5)
Ghosts, beings (7)
Gift from Mary to Elizabeth (6)
Giles (5)
God's house (6)
He arrests Elizabeth (7)
He was an expert spirit remover (4)
If Proctor tells the truth, he will save his (4)
John; he tries to make people see the truth (7)
Many of Mrs. Putnam's have died (6)
Material proof (8)
Meeting place of Tituba and the devil (6)
Method of execution using a rope (4)
Move with rhythm (5)
Mr. Corey (5)
Mr. Nurse (7)
Mrs. Nurse (7)
Object of the Putnams' dispute with the
Nurses (4)
One who tells the truth is this (6)
Opposite of bad (4)
Parris wanted a deed and this along with his salary (8)
Parris' daughter (5)
Parris' slave woman from Barbados (6)
Play division (3)
Reading material (5)
Rebecca (5)
Rebecca is full of it (8)
Satan (5)
She is the primary cause of the witch hunts (7)
She wants Abby to tell the truth (4)
Something that shows the existence of a fact (4)
Story written to be performed on the stage (4)
The Creator (3)
The act of pretending (8)
The christian holy book (5)
The commandment Proctor forgets (8)
Thomas Putnam was this about his situation in life (6)
To adore (7)
Woman who pracitces witchcraft (5)

The Crucible Word Search 2 Answer Key

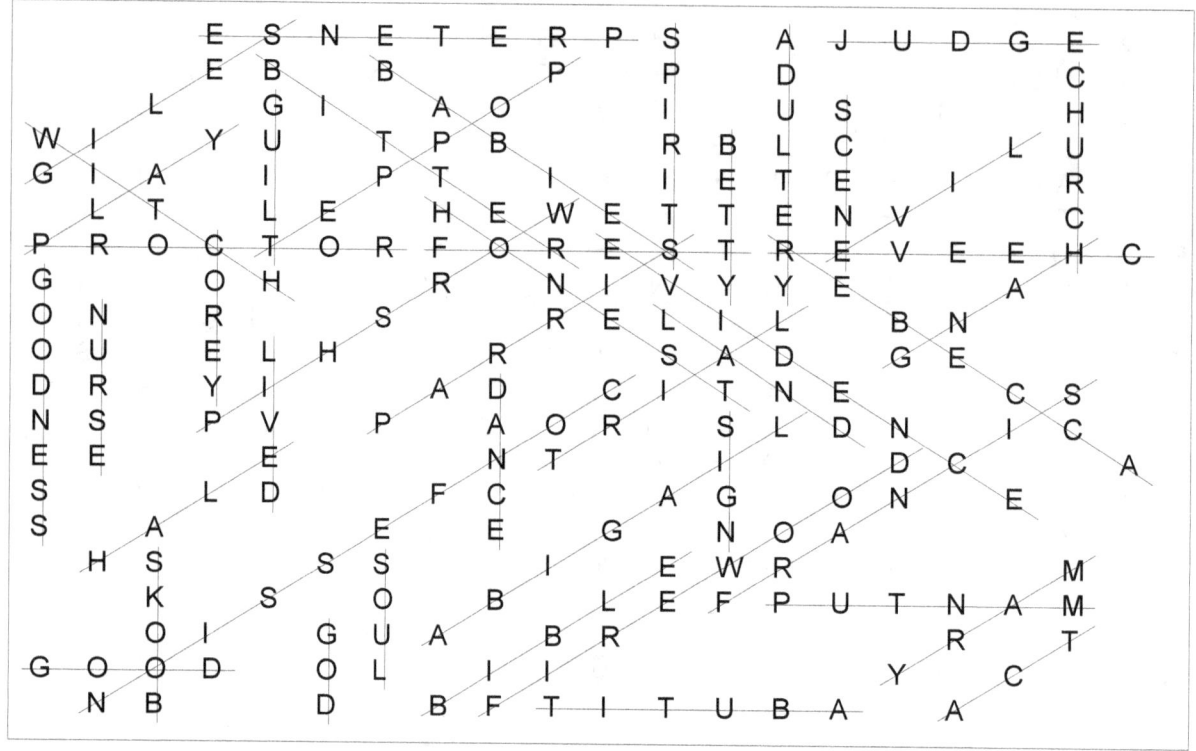

Admission (10)
Ann or Thomas (6)
Bad (4)
Betty's father and Abigail's uncle (6)
Conscience's nagging feeling (5)
Decision maker in court (5)
Division of an act (5)
Examination of evidence to determine guilt or innocence (5)
Ghosts, beings (7)
Gift from Mary to Elizabeth (6)
Giles (5)
God's house (6)
He arrests Elizabeth (7)
He was an expert spirit remover (4)
If Proctor tells the truth, he will save his (4)
John; he tries to make people see the truth (7)
Many of Mrs. Putnam's have died (6)
Material proof (8)
Meeting place of Tituba and the devil (6)
Method of execution using a rope (4)
Move with rhythm (5)
Mr. Corey (5)
Mr. Nurse (7)
Mrs. Nurse (7)
Object of the Putnams' dispute with the

Nurses (4)
One who tells the truth is this (6)
Opposite of bad (4)
Parris wanted a deed and this along with his salary (8)
Parris' daughter (5)
Parris' slave woman from Barbados (6)
Play division (3)
Reading material (5)
Rebecca (5)
Rebecca is full of it (8)
Satan (5)
She is the primary cause of the witch hunts (7)
She wants Abby to tell the truth (4)
Something that shows the existence of a fact (4)
Story written to be performed on the stage (4)
The Creator (3)
The act of pretending (8)
The christian holy book (5)
The commandment Proctor forgets (8)
Thomas Putnam was this about his situation in life (6)
To adore (7)
Woman who pracitces witchcraft (5)

The Crucible Word Search 3

W	C	B	S	B	P	V	S	E	L	I	G	F	F	P	E	C	M	P	V
P	I	H	I	O	J	D	P	V	L	H	C	R	I	N	L	A	R	A	Z
T	N	T	U	B	U	P	I	S	C	S	A	H	R	R	N	D	N	R	X
G	C	A	C	R	L	L	R	V	V	N	S	O	G	T	E	O	B	R	H
C	J	D	C	H	C	E	I	G	C	R	H	S	U	V	I	W	B	I	S
J	J	U	O	X	C	H	T	I	O	T	B	P	I	S	Q	J	O	S	S
M	Q	L	M	K	X	R	S	W	W	B	T	L	S	D	Y	P	E	O	D
K	G	T	M	J	G	X	A	A	P	S	L	E	B	J	P	N	D	C	D
S	F	E	A	K	G	B	H	F	Q	D	F	Y	N	V	D	S	M	C	W
F	G	R	N	W	S	A	K	R	T	N	Q	L	C	O	N	C	F	X	D
D	B	Y	D	L	C	B	X	F	O	S	D	D	O	O	B	E	M	B	K
A	M	B	M	C	V	P	J	C	Q	L	G	G	F	N	R	N	R	I	D
N	N	N	E	H	P	Y	O	H	T	E	B	A	Z	I	L	E	N	T	F
F	B	B	N	A	D	R	R	P	T	Y	W	X	Z	J	V	M	Y	T	M
O	E	D	T	N	N	T	E	K	P	X	H	P	D	E	L	X	A	E	J
R	R	L	S	G	B	E	T	T	Y	E	C	N	E	D	I	V	E	R	V
T	F	N	I	X	J	H	C	R	E	R	T	H	L	N	A	Z	S	D	Y
H	J	S	R	P	U	A	G	I	Y	N	C	P	D	J	G	N	Q	C	D
R	P	K	W	B	D	N	W	A	G	B	S	I	H	R	I	B	C	O	F
E	V	I	L	D	G	U	I	L	T	O	V	E	O	R	B	A	G	E	P
W	F	H	N	X	E	X	T	D	B	I	O	T	N	Y	A	B	H	S	J
R	F	A	A	R	Y	F	C	M	D	H	C	D	E	X	P	I	D	R	Y
J	L	H	Q	L	F	S	H	U	B	O	O	K	S	Q	L	E	J	U	J
G	Y	N	G	C	E	D	A	D	R	Y	D	F	T	M	A	S	J	N	V
F	O	R	E	S	T	L	M	P	T	I	T	U	B	A	Y	W	F	C	C

ABIGAIL	DANCE	GUILT	PRETENSE
ACT	DANFORTH	HALE	PROCTOR
ADULTERY	DEVIL	HANG	PUTNAM
BABIES	ELIZABETH	HAWTHORNE	REBECCA
BETTY	EVIDENCE	HONEST	SCENE
BIBLE	EVIL	INDIVIDUAL	SIGN
BITTER	FIREWOOD	JUDGE	SOUL
BOOKS	FOREST	LAND	SPIRITS
CHEEVER	FRANCIS	MARY	TITUBA
CHURCH	GILES	NURSE	TRIAL
COMMANDMENTS	GOD	PARRIS	WITCH
CONFESSION	GOOD	PLAY	WITCHCRAFT
COREY	GOODNESS	POPPET	WORSHIP

The Crucible Word Search 3 Answer Key

ABIGAIL	DANCE	GUILT	PRETENSE
ACT	DANFORTH	HALE	PROCTOR
ADULTERY	DEVIL	HANG	PUTNAM
BABIES	ELIZABETH	HAWTHORNE	REBECCA
BETTY	EVIDENCE	HONEST	SCENE
BIBLE	EVIL	INDIVIDUAL	SIGN
BITTER	FIREWOOD	JUDGE	SOUL
BOOKS	FOREST	LAND	SPIRITS
CHEEVER	FRANCIS	MARY	TITUBA
CHURCH	GILES	NURSE	TRIAL
COMMANDMENTS	GOD	PARRIS	WITCH
CONFESSION	GOOD	PLAY	WITCHCRAFT
COREY	GOODNESS	POPPET	WORSHIP

The Crucible Word Search 4

```
C H E E V E R D E I N D I V I D U A L V
H G R B J K H S B N R Y Q G T S W K L S
S G O S S T N E M D N A M M O C I H B N
N F T Q L E V D N G X L L N K E T V F G
X J C V T W O R S H I P G J K L C T F Y
L P O E N L N X S S Y F O V C I H W I P
Y R R D V Y B J V B M M O H Y Z C Y R M
J P P Y C L T T D F F A D C M A R B E Z
U T P T N G Y M D B D N N O B A I W G
D K C T J E S Y N Z K T E R F E F B O R
G P D E X E V P A T K U S E F T T L O C
E T A B I G A I L L M P S Y D H R E D B
D P T B I C X I L A O P O T L C I Y N
X A A M C T U D R P Y H O R U N K K A X
Z B N E J G T Y P P B G O J E L D C P L
X T B C H A L E F G A F Y D A C T N W T
T E N O E Y T S R A N R I O Q N G T J Y
R N L N W R T R B A B V R G C I T P Y H
V R R F B I F U D D E O D I S H K V Q W
F O R E S T T N N U N H O K S G U S J Z
S H W S X I S C D L J N R K L N I R T L
W T X S T D E G H T L N D I S A V L C D
V W Y I P M N S C E N E V Y N H M C E H
V A G O Z J O L W R R E F R A N C I S S
K H M N Q M H L J Y D S P I R I T S W B
```

ABIGAIL	DANCE	GUILT	PRETENSE
ACT	DANFORTH	HALE	PROCTOR
ADULTERY	DEVIL	HANG	PUTNAM
BABIES	ELIZABETH	HAWTHORNE	REBECCA
BETTY	EVIDENCE	HONEST	SCENE
BIBLE	EVIL	INDIVIDUAL	SIGN
BITTER	FIREWOOD	JUDGE	SOUL
BOOKS	FOREST	LAND	SPIRITS
CHEEVER	FRANCIS	MARY	TITUBA
CHURCH	GILES	NURSE	TRIAL
COMMANDMENTS	GOD	PARRIS	WITCH
CONFESSION	GOOD	PLAY	WITCHCRAFT
COREY	GOODNESS	POPPET	WORSHIP

The Crucible Word Search 4 Answer Key

ABIGAIL	DANCE	GUILT	PRETENSE
ACT	DANFORTH	HALE	PROCTOR
ADULTERY	DEVIL	HANG	PUTNAM
BABIES	ELIZABETH	HAWTHORNE	REBECCA
BETTY	EVIDENCE	HONEST	SCENE
BIBLE	EVIL	INDIVIDUAL	SIGN
BITTER	FIREWOOD	JUDGE	SOUL
BOOKS	FOREST	LAND	SPIRITS
CHEEVER	FRANCIS	MARY	TITUBA
CHURCH	GILES	NURSE	TRIAL
COMMANDMENTS	GOD	PARRIS	WITCH
CONFESSION	GOOD	PLAY	WITCHCRAFT
COREY	GOODNESS	POPPET	WORSHIP

The Crucible Crossword 1

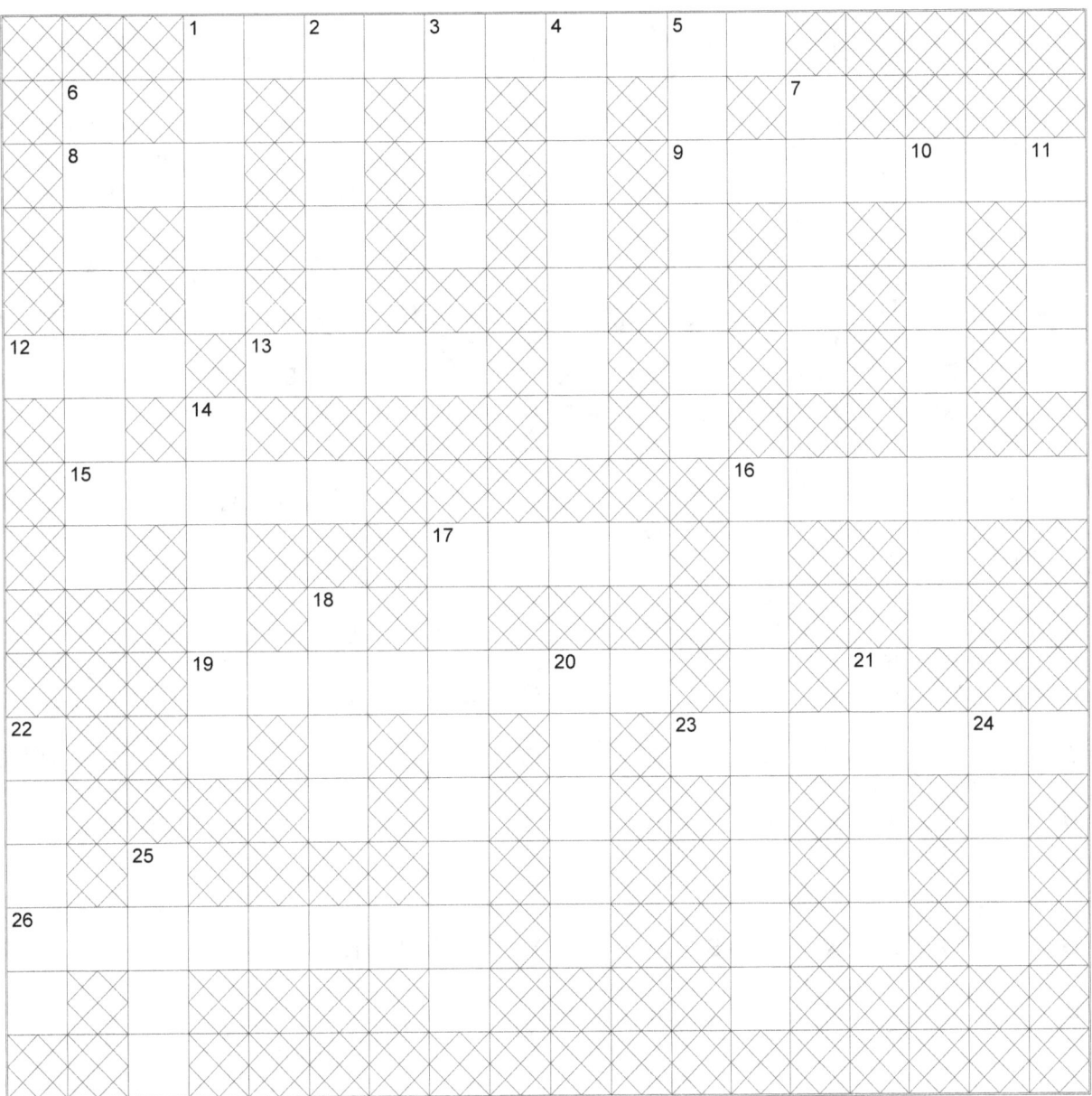

Across
1. Black magic; sorcery
8. Play division
9. She is the primary cause of the witch hunts
12. The Creator
13. She wants Abby to tell the truth
15. Examination of evidence to determine guilt or innocence
16. One who tells the truth is this
17. Story written to be performed on the stage
19. Material proof
23. He arrests Elizabeth
26. Rebecca is full of it

Down
1. Woman who pracitces witchcraft
2. Parris' slave woman from Barbados
3. He was an expert spirit remover
4. Mrs. Nurse
5. Mr. Nurse
6. The judge for many witchcraft trials
7. The christian holy book
10. The commandment Proctor forgets
11. Object of the Putnams' dispute with the Nurses
14. Thomas Putnam was this about his situation in life
16. He thinks of a test for Mary
17. The act of pretending
18. Something that shows the existence of a fact
20. Giles
21. Parris' daughter
22. Decision maker in court
24. Bad
25. If Proctor tells the truth, he will save his

The Crucible Crossword 1 Answer Key

			1 W	I	2 T	C	3 H	C	4 R	A	5 F	T			
		6 D	I		I		A		E		R		7 B		
		8 A	C	T	T		L		B		9 A	B	I	10 G	A	11 I	L
		N	C		U		E		E		N		B		D		A
		F	H		B				C		C		L		U		N
12 G	O	D		13 M	A	R	Y		C		I		E		L		D
		R		14 B					A		S				T		
		15 T	R	I	A	L					16 H	O	N	E	S	T
		H		T			17 P	L	A	Y		A			R		
				T		18 S		R				A W			Y		
				19 E	V	I	D	E	N	20 C	E		21 B				
22 J		R				G		T		O		23 C	H	E	E	24 V	E	R
U						N		E		R		H		O		T		V
D		25 S						N		E		O		R		T		I
26 G	O	O	D	N	E	S	S		Y			N		Y		L
E		U				E						E				
		L														

Across
1. Black magic; sorcery
8. Play division
9. She is the primary cause of the witch hunts
12. The Creator
13. She wants Abby to tell the truth
15. Examination of evidence to determine guilt or innocence
16. One who tells the truth is this
17. Story written to be performed on the stage
19. Material proof
23. He arrests Elizabeth
26. Rebecca is full of it

Down
1. Woman who pracitces witchcraft
2. Parris' slave woman from Barbados
3. He was an expert spirit remover
4. Mrs. Nurse
5. Mr. Nurse
6. The judge for many witchcraft trials
7. The christian holy book
10. The commandment Proctor forgets
11. Object of the Putnams' dispute with the Nurses
14. Thomas Putnam was this about his situation in life
16. He thinks of a test for Mary
17. The act of pretending
18. Something that shows the existence of a fact
20. Giles
21. Parris' daughter
22. Decision maker in court
24. Bad
25. If Proctor tells the truth, he will save his

The Crucible Crossword 2

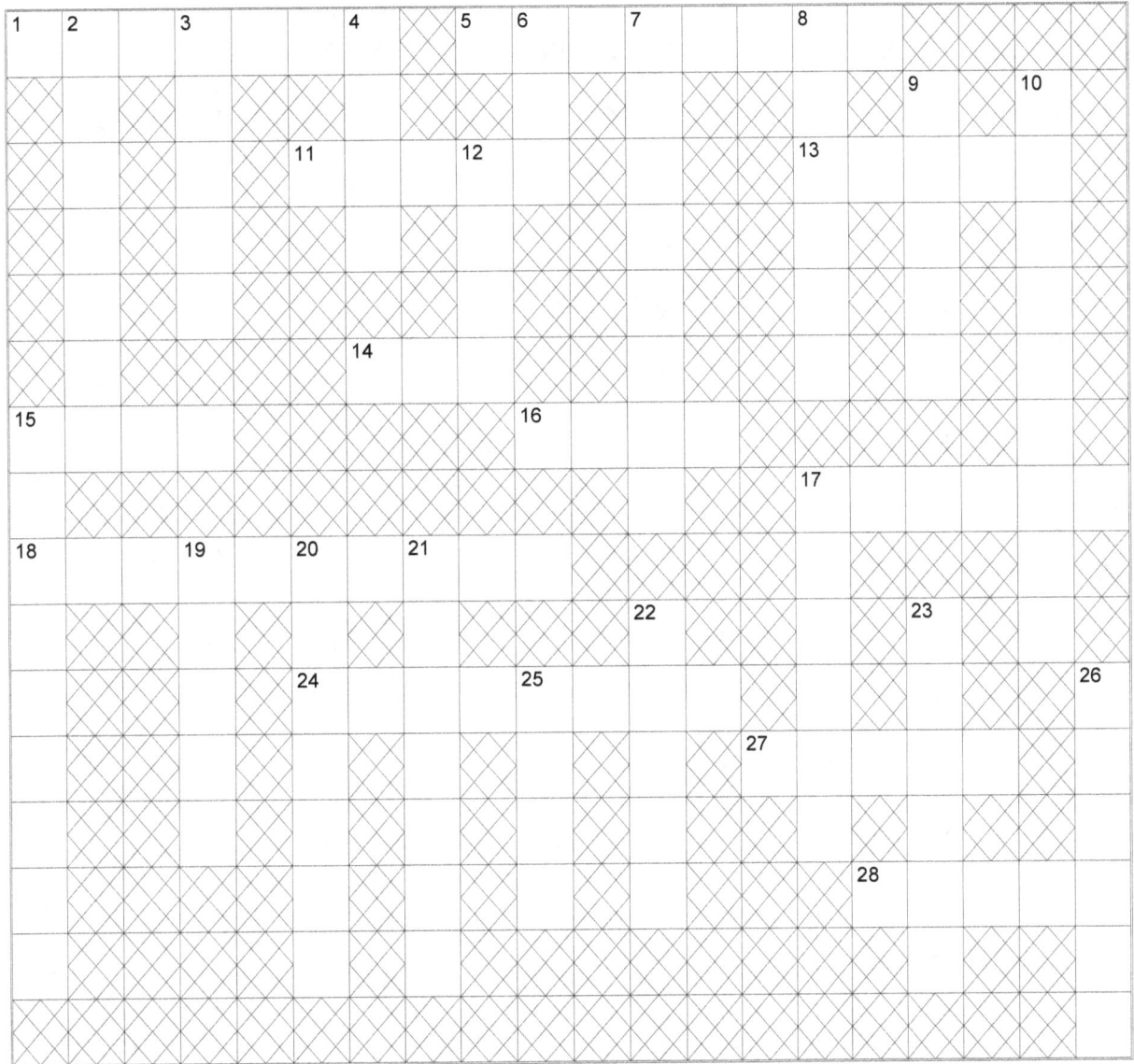

Across
1. Mr. Nurse
5. The judge for many witchcraft trials
11. Conscience's nagging feeling
13. Examination of evidence to determine guilt or innocence
14. The Creator
15. He was an expert spirit remover
16. Opposite of bad
17. Thomas Putnam was this about his situation in life
18. Black magic; sorcery
24. Material proof
27. Parris' daughter
28. Move with rhythm

Down
2. Mrs. Nurse
3. Rebecca
4. If Proctor tells the truth, he will save his
6. Play division
7. Parris wanted a deed and this along with his salary
8. Parris' slave woman from Barbados
9. The christian holy book
10. John's wife
12. Object of the Putnams' dispute with the Nurses
15. He thinks of a test for Mary
17. Many of Mrs. Putnam's have died
19. Giles
20. He arrests Elizabeth
21. She is the primary cause of the witch hunts
22. Division of an act
23. Ann or Thomas
25. Bad
26. One who tells the truth is this

The Crucible Crossword 2 Answer Key

	1 F	2 R	3 A	N	4 C	I	5 S		6 D	A	N	7 F	O	R	8 T	H		
		E		U			O		C			I			I		9 B	10 E
		B		R	11 G	U	I	12 L	T			R		13 T	R	I	A	L
		E		S			L	A				E		U		B		I
		C		E				N				W		B		L		Z
		C			14 G	O	D					O		A		E		A
15 H	A	L	E						16 G	O	O	D						B
A									D					17 B	I	T	T	E	R
18 W	I	19 T	C	20 H	C	21 R	A	F	T					A				T
T		O		H		B						22 S		B		23 P		H
H		R		24 E	V	I	D	25 E	N	C	E			I		U		26 H
O		E		E		G		V			E		27 B	E	T	T	Y	O
R		Y		V		A		I			N		S			N		N
N				E		I		L			E		28 D	A	N	C	E	
E						L							M					S
																		T

Across
1. Mr. Nurse
5. The judge for many witchcraft trials
11. Conscience's nagging feeling
13. Examination of evidence to determine guilt or innocence
14. The Creator
15. He was an expert spirit remover
16. Opposite of bad
17. Thomas Putnam was this about his situation in life
18. Black magic; sorcery
24. Material proof
27. Parris' daughter
28. Move with rhythm

Down
2. Mrs. Nurse
3. Rebecca
4. If Proctor tells the truth, he will save his
6. Play division
7. Parris wanted a deed and this along with his salary
8. Parris' slave woman from Barbados
9. The christian holy book
10. John's wife
12. Object of the Putnams' dispute with the Nurses
15. He thinks of a test for Mary
17. Many of Mrs. Putnam's have died
19. Giles
20. He arrests Elizabeth
21. She is the primary cause of the witch hunts
22. Division of an act
23. Ann or Thomas
25. Bad
26. One who tells the truth is this

The Crucible Crossword 3

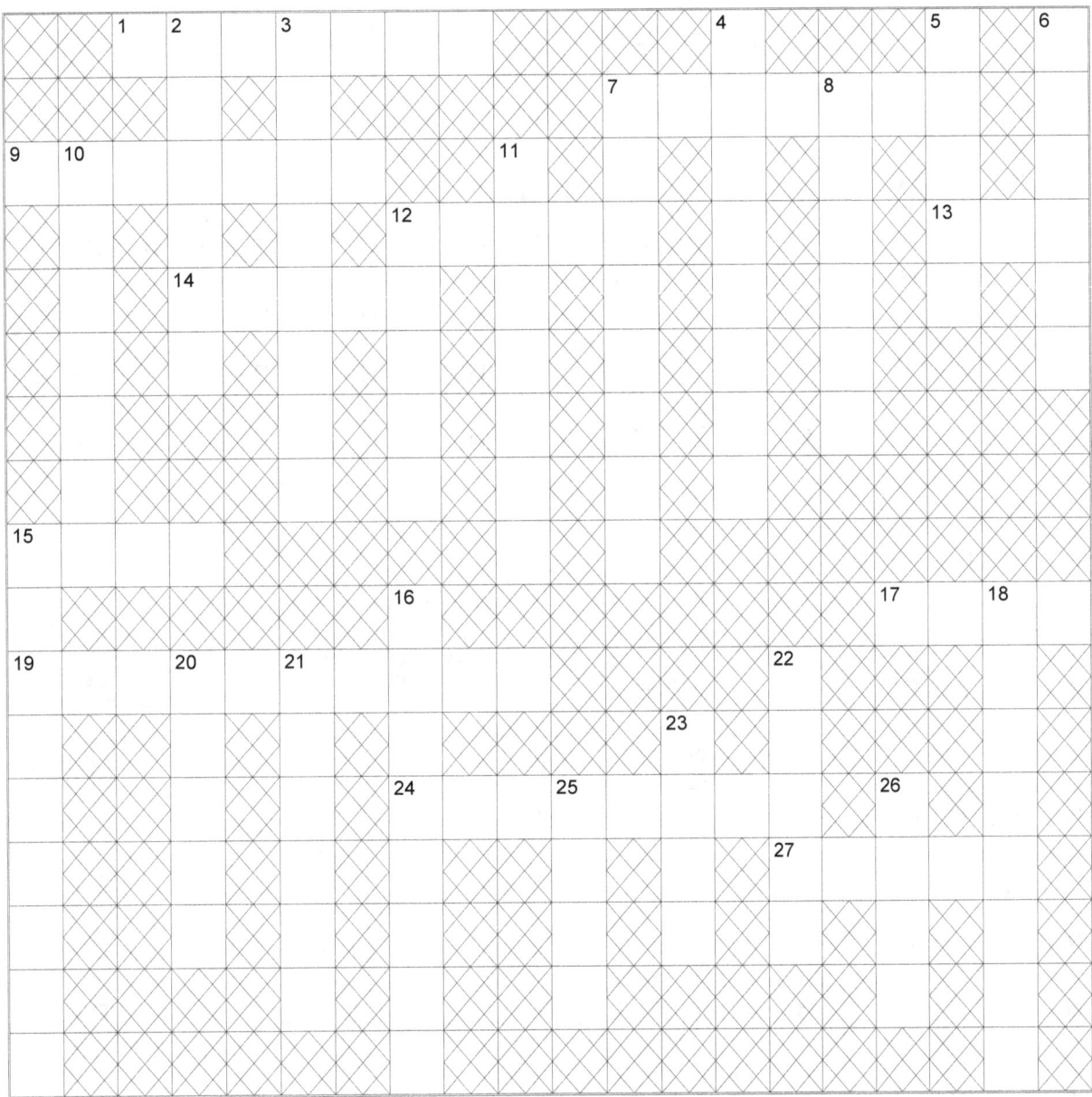

Across
1. He arrests Elizabeth
7. John; he tries to make people see the truth
9. Mr. Nurse
12. The christian holy book
13. Play division
14. Division of an act
15. He was an expert spirit remover
17. Story written to be performed on the stage
19. Black magic; sorcery
24. Parris wanted a deed and this along with his salary
27. Conscience's nagging feeling

Down
2. One who tells the truth is this
3. Material proof
4. Rebecca is full of it
5. Examination of evidence to determine guilt or innocence
6. Thomas Putnam was this about his situation in life
7. The act of pretending
8. Parris' slave woman from Barbados
10. Mrs. Nurse
11. She is the primary cause of the witch hunts
12. Parris' daughter
15. He thinks of a test for Mary
16. The judge for many witchcraft trials
18. The commandment Proctor forgets
20. Giles
21. God's house
22. Decision maker in court
23. If Proctor tells the truth, he will save his
25. Bad
26. Something that shows the existence of a fact

The Crucible Crossword 3 Answer Key

Across
1. He arrests Elizabeth
7. John; he tries to make people see the truth
9. Mr. Nurse
12. The christian holy book
13. Play division
14. Division of an act
15. He was an expert spirit remover
17. Story written to be performed on the stage
19. Black magic; sorcery
24. Parris wanted a deed and this along with his salary
27. Conscience's nagging feeling

Down
2. One who tells the truth is this
3. Material proof
4. Rebecca is full of it
5. Examination of evidence to determine guilt or innocence
6. Thomas Putnam was this about his situation in life
7. The act of pretending
8. Parris' slave woman from Barbados
10. Mrs. Nurse
11. She is the primary cause of the witch hunts
12. Parris' daughter
15. He thinks of a test for Mary
16. The judge for many witchcraft trials
18. The commandment Proctor forgets
20. Giles
21. God's house
22. Decision maker in court
23. If Proctor tells the truth, he will save his
25. Bad
26. Something that shows the existence of a fact

The Crucible Crossword 4

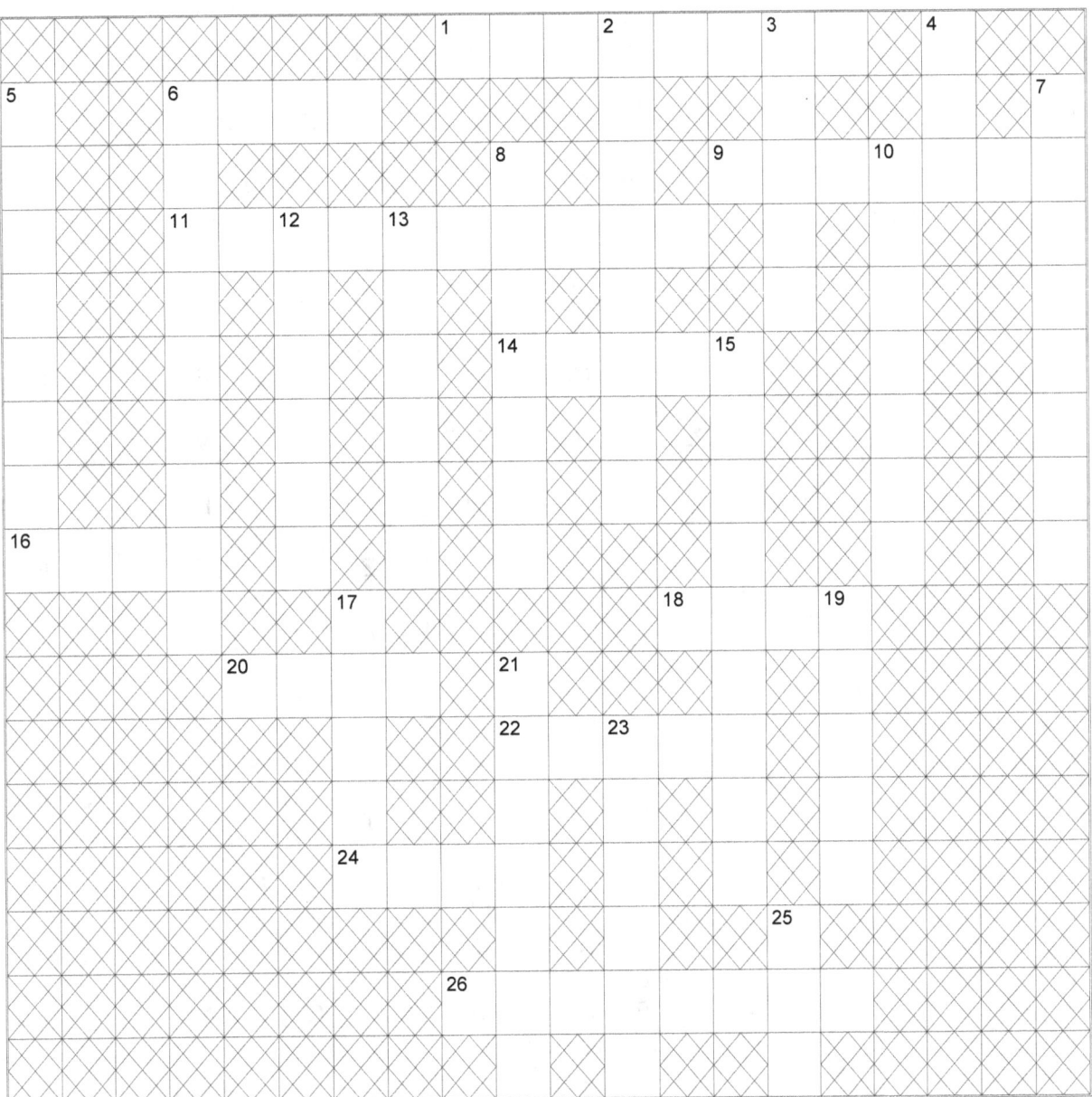

Across
1. Material proof
6. He was an expert spirit remover
9. John; he tries to make people see the truth
11. Black magic; sorcery
14. Rebecca
16. Something that shows the existence of a fact
18. Object of the Putnams' dispute with the Nurses
20. Bad
22. The christian holy book
24. Method of execution using a rope
26. Parris wanted a deed and this along with his salary

Down
2. The judge for many witchcraft trials
3. Giles
4. Play division
5. Rebecca is full of it
6. He thinks of a test for Mary
7. The act of pretending
8. Mr. Nurse
10. He arrests Elizabeth
12. Parris' slave woman from Barbados
13. One who tells the truth is this
15. John's wife
17. Woman who pracitces witchcraft
19. Move with rhythm
21. She is the primary cause of the witch hunts
23. Thomas Putnam was this about his situation in life
25. The Creator

The Crucible Crossword 4 Answer Key

						1 E	2 V	I	D	E	N	3 C	E		4 A		
5 G		6 H	A	L	E				A			O			C		7 P
O		A					8 F		N		9 P	R	O	10 C	T	O	R
O		11 W	12 I	13 T	C	H	C	R	A	F	T			H			E
D		T		I		O			A		O			Y		E		T
N		H		T		N		14 N	U	R	S	15 E			E		E
E		O		U		E		C			T		L			V		N
S		R		B		S		I			H		I			E		S
16 S	I	G	N	A		T		S					Z			R		E
				E		17 W					18 L	A	19 N	D	
			20 E	V	I	L		21 A					B		A		
				T				22 B	I	23 B	L	E			N		
				C				I		I				T		C	
				24 H	A	N	G			T		H			E	
								A		T		25 G			
				26 F	I	R	E	W	O	O	D				
								L		R		D				

Across
1. Material proof
6. He was an expert spirit remover
9. John; he tries to make people see the truth
11. Black magic; sorcery
14. Rebecca
16. Something that shows the existence of a fact
18. Object of the Putnams' dispute with the Nurses
20. Bad
22. The christian holy book
24. Method of execution using a rope
26. Parris wanted a deed and this along with his salary

5. Rebecca is full of it
6. He thinks of a test for Mary
7. The act of pretending
8. Mr. Nurse
10. He arrests Elizabeth
12. Parris' slave woman from Barbados
13. One who tells the truth is this
15. John's wife
17. Woman who pracitces witchcraft
19. Move with rhythm
21. She is the primary cause of the witch hunts
23. Thomas Putnam was this about his situation in life
25. The Creator

Down
2. The judge for many witchcraft trials
3. Giles
4. Play division

The Crucible

CONFESSION	HAWTHORNE	ELIZABETH	FRANCIS	BABIES
MARY	BITTER	COREY	PUTNAM	CHURCH
HALE	PROCTOR	FREE SPACE	HONEST	WORSHIP
BIBLE	DANCE	WITCH	PLAY	GOD
GOODNESS	NURSE	LAND	HANG	CHEEVER

The Crucible

BETTY	GILES	FIREWOOD	INDIVIDUAL	DANFORTH
REBECCA	DEVIL	GUILT	POPPET	COMMANDMENTS
WITCHCRAFT	GOOD	FREE SPACE	BOOKS	PARRIS
TRIAL	PRETENSE	FOREST	EVIDENCE	SOUL
EVIL	SIGN	TITUBA	ABIGAIL	ACT

The Crucible

BETTY	BIBLE	LAND	TITUBA	PROCTOR
SOUL	FRANCIS	SPIRITS	PLAY	PUTNAM
WORSHIP	HANG	FREE SPACE	INDIVIDUAL	HAWTHORNE
FIREWOOD	HONEST	FOREST	PARRIS	REBECCA
ACT	DANFORTH	DEVIL	MARY	POPPET

The Crucible

ABIGAIL	BITTER	JUDGE	ADULTERY	WITCH
COREY	CHURCH	GOD	BOOKS	CHEEVER
GUILT	CONFESSION	FREE SPACE	HALE	NURSE
EVIL	WITCHCRAFT	COMMANDMENTS	GILES	TRIAL
BABIES	SIGN	PRETENSE	DANCE	EVIDENCE

The Crucible

GILES	BABIES	GOD	BETTY	NURSE
HANG	SOUL	GOOD	SPIRITS	BOOKS
INDIVIDUAL	MARY	FREE SPACE	ADULTERY	GOODNESS
POPPET	CHEEVER	HONEST	BIBLE	WITCHCRAFT
TITUBA	LAND	DANFORTH	BITTER	HAWTHORNE

The Crucible

PARRIS	JUDGE	COMMANDMENTS	WORSHIP	EVIL
ELIZABETH	CONFESSION	ABIGAIL	REBECCA	SIGN
EVIDENCE	COREY	FREE SPACE	ACT	TRIAL
WITCH	PLAY	HALE	DANCE	GUILT
FIREWOOD	PRETENSE	PUTNAM	FOREST	FRANCIS

The Crucible

WORSHIP	PLAY	HAWTHORNE	PARRIS	CONFESSION
TITUBA	GOD	PRETENSE	HONEST	FIREWOOD
DANCE	WITCHCRAFT	FREE SPACE	FOREST	SCENE
POPPET	BETTY	PROCTOR	REBECCA	SIGN
NURSE	LAND	ACT	FRANCIS	COMMANDMENTS

The Crucible

COREY	BIBLE	GOOD	INDIVIDUAL	BABIES
PUTNAM	EVIL	TRIAL	GOODNESS	ADULTERY
GILES	EVIDENCE	FREE SPACE	HALE	BITTER
CHEEVER	ELIZABETH	JUDGE	DANFORTH	MARY
SPIRITS	DEVIL	WITCH	GUILT	BOOKS

Copyrighted

The Crucible

HAWTHORNE	SOUL	DANFORTH	HALE	NURSE
FRANCIS	BETTY	PUTNAM	BOOKS	HONEST
ACT	BIBLE	FREE SPACE	COREY	INDIVIDUAL
DEVIL	GOD	SIGN	PROCTOR	POPPET
PLAY	WORSHIP	SCENE	PARRIS	DANCE

The Crucible

JUDGE	EVIDENCE	MARY	GOODNESS	CONFESSION
LAND	BABIES	CHURCH	TRIAL	GILES
EVIL	CHEEVER	FREE SPACE	COMMANDMENTS	PRETENSE
FOREST	SPIRITS	BITTER	WITCHCRAFT	FIREWOOD
REBECCA	ADULTERY	WITCH	GUILT	ELIZABETH

The Crucible

WITCHCRAFT	BIBLE	PLAY	EVIL	WORSHIP
NURSE	DANFORTH	GILES	CONFESSION	PROCTOR
BABIES	HAWTHORNE	FREE SPACE	TITUBA	COMMANDMENTS
GOD	PUTNAM	POPPET	GOOD	PRETENSE
FRANCIS	HALE	SCENE	SIGN	COREY

The Crucible

MARY	PARRIS	CHURCH	BOOKS	CHEEVER
WITCH	HONEST	SOUL	FIREWOOD	GOODNESS
BETTY	INDIVIDUAL	FREE SPACE	DEVIL	HANG
SPIRITS	ABIGAIL	TRIAL	ADULTERY	ACT
GUILT	ELIZABETH	EVIDENCE	BITTER	LAND

The Crucible

SOUL	EVIL	PARRIS	INDIVIDUAL	SPIRITS
DEVIL	HONEST	SCENE	ABIGAIL	LAND
TITUBA	WITCHCRAFT	FREE SPACE	FOREST	DANFORTH
GOOD	NURSE	TRIAL	GUILT	JUDGE
DANCE	PRETENSE	FRANCIS	WORSHIP	PUTNAM

The Crucible

PLAY	HALE	BOOKS	ADULTERY	COREY
BITTER	GOD	FIREWOOD	BABIES	POPPET
COMMANDMENTS	ACT	FREE SPACE	CHURCH	GOODNESS
PROCTOR	WITCH	CHEEVER	MARY	BIBLE
SIGN	CONFESSION	ELIZABETH	HAWTHORNE	HANG

The Crucible

EVIL	FOREST	COREY	BITTER	ABIGAIL
GOOD	BETTY	GILES	PUTNAM	REBECCA
SCENE	COMMANDMENTS	FREE SPACE	CONFESSION	FIREWOOD
FRANCIS	INDIVIDUAL	SPIRITS	JUDGE	PLAY
WITCHCRAFT	SOUL	EVIDENCE	CHURCH	HONEST

The Crucible

BABIES	TITUBA	ELIZABETH	DANFORTH	LAND
ADULTERY	HAWTHORNE	BOOKS	BIBLE	GOD
WITCH	NURSE	FREE SPACE	DEVIL	CHEEVER
DANCE	GUILT	PRETENSE	PROCTOR	SIGN
GOODNESS	HALE	TRIAL	ACT	MARY

The Crucible

BITTER	GUILT	EVIDENCE	FRANCIS	CHEEVER
PLAY	NURSE	MARY	FOREST	TITUBA
SIGN	CHURCH	FREE SPACE	GOD	INDIVIDUAL
EVIL	HANG	WORSHIP	DANFORTH	PARRIS
GILES	WITCH	TRIAL	HONEST	SCENE

The Crucible

BOOKS	DANCE	HALE	BIBLE	SPIRITS
JUDGE	ACT	ELIZABETH	LAND	GOOD
ABIGAIL	BABIES	FREE SPACE	DEVIL	SOUL
PUTNAM	COREY	BETTY	PROCTOR	WITCHCRAFT
ADULTERY	PRETENSE	COMMANDMENTS	CONFESSION	FIREWOOD

The Crucible

GOOD	POPPET	PROCTOR	PUTNAM	ACT
SIGN	FRANCIS	SCENE	PARRIS	CONFESSION
ELIZABETH	DANFORTH	FREE SPACE	TRIAL	PLAY
COREY	GOD	TITUBA	BOOKS	ABIGAIL
GILES	HONEST	DANCE	REBECCA	WITCH

The Crucible

FIREWOOD	HALE	GOODNESS	NURSE	INDIVIDUAL
PRETENSE	JUDGE	HANG	EVIL	WORSHIP
BITTER	ADULTERY	FREE SPACE	BABIES	BIBLE
EVIDENCE	CHURCH	LAND	WITCHCRAFT	CHEEVER
COMMANDMENTS	MARY	GUILT	SOUL	BETTY

The Crucible

JUDGE	HALE	COREY	FRANCIS	HONEST
SCENE	PROCTOR	FOREST	ABIGAIL	CHEEVER
GUILT	DANCE	FREE SPACE	EVIL	TRIAL
GOOD	BOOKS	BABIES	ADULTERY	COMMANDMENTS
BETTY	BITTER	INDIVIDUAL	ACT	PARRIS

The Crucible

BIBLE	WORSHIP	SOUL	DANFORTH	GOODNESS
HAWTHORNE	EVIDENCE	WITCH	CONFESSION	CHURCH
POPPET	HANG	FREE SPACE	SPIRITS	ELIZABETH
MARY	REBECCA	GOD	LAND	FIREWOOD
DEVIL	TITUBA	NURSE	GILES	PRETENSE

The Crucible

BABIES	FRANCIS	WORSHIP	DANCE	NURSE
SOUL	TITUBA	HANG	PRETENSE	ELIZABETH
DEVIL	CHURCH	FREE SPACE	ADULTERY	GOOD
TRIAL	WITCH	REBECCA	HAWTHORNE	CHEEVER
JUDGE	EVIDENCE	LAND	CONFESSION	EVIL

The Crucible

SPIRITS	ACT	PROCTOR	SIGN	GOD
PUTNAM	MARY	BOOKS	PLAY	WITCHCRAFT
COMMANDMENTS	BETTY	FREE SPACE	COREY	GUILT
GILES	PARRIS	HALE	BITTER	POPPET
BIBLE	GOODNESS	FOREST	DANFORTH	SCENE

The Crucible

GOODNESS	ACT	HAWTHORNE	INDIVIDUAL	SIGN
GOOD	SCENE	POPPET	FRANCIS	ABIGAIL
FIREWOOD	PARRIS	FREE SPACE	ELIZABETH	PRETENSE
EVIDENCE	SOUL	BETTY	MARY	CONFESSION
CHEEVER	EVIL	GILES	TITUBA	BITTER

The Crucible

PROCTOR	PLAY	BIBLE	HALE	LAND
BOOKS	WITCHCRAFT	FOREST	COMMANDMENTS	HANG
DEVIL	NURSE	FREE SPACE	GUILT	SPIRITS
BABIES	WITCH	CHURCH	HONEST	TRIAL
DANFORTH	COREY	ADULTERY	PUTNAM	DANCE

The Crucible

COREY	PUTNAM	NURSE	BIBLE	HALE
DANCE	GOD	INDIVIDUAL	EVIDENCE	HAWTHORNE
JUDGE	HONEST	FREE SPACE	CONFESSION	TITUBA
BITTER	REBECCA	SCENE	FRANCIS	POPPET
CHEEVER	FOREST	DANFORTH	BOOKS	SIGN

The Crucible

SOUL	MARY	PLAY	ACT	PARRIS
PRETENSE	GOOD	ABIGAIL	TRIAL	FIREWOOD
CHURCH	GUILT	FREE SPACE	GILES	BETTY
PROCTOR	ADULTERY	SPIRITS	GOODNESS	WITCH
DEVIL	LAND	ELIZABETH	WITCHCRAFT	COMMANDMENTS

The Crucible

CHURCH	JUDGE	SPIRITS	DANFORTH	GOD
COREY	PLAY	WITCH	BOOKS	DANCE
NURSE	PROCTOR	FREE SPACE	LAND	CONFESSION
ADULTERY	EVIL	DEVIL	PARRIS	PRETENSE
COMMANDMENTS	GUILT	BIBLE	ABIGAIL	SOUL

The Crucible

GOODNESS	PUTNAM	FOREST	WORSHIP	HANG
POPPET	SIGN	HONEST	CHEEVER	FRANCIS
TRIAL	HALE	FREE SPACE	ACT	BETTY
INDIVIDUAL	GOOD	EVIDENCE	MARY	HAWTHORNE
REBECCA	TITUBA	ELIZABETH	WITCHCRAFT	BITTER

The Crucible

EVIDENCE	BABIES	JUDGE	BETTY	INDIVIDUAL
COMMANDMENTS	ABIGAIL	TITUBA	CONFESSION	WITCH
GILES	MARY	FREE SPACE	HANG	DEVIL
FOREST	DANCE	ADULTERY	BIBLE	LAND
HONEST	FIREWOOD	POPPET	GOD	DANFORTH

The Crucible

REBECCA	ELIZABETH	TRIAL	BITTER	ACT
EVIL	HAWTHORNE	GOOD	FRANCIS	SOUL
WORSHIP	COREY	FREE SPACE	SIGN	WITCHCRAFT
PARRIS	GOODNESS	HALE	PROCTOR	PRETENSE
GUILT	CHURCH	SPIRITS	NURSE	CHEEVER

The Crucible Vocabulary Word List

No. Word	Clue/Definition
1. ABOMINATIONS	Things that elicit great dislike or abhorrence
2. ADAMANT	Firm in purpose or opinion; unyielding
3. ALLEGIANCE	Loyalty
4. ANARCHY	Political disorder and confusion
5. ANONYMITY	Secrecy; having unknown or unacknowledged name
6. ANTAGONISTS	Adversaries; opponents
7. ASCERTAIN	Find out
8. AUDIBLE	Able to be heard
9. AVIDLY	Enthusiastically
10. BASE	Having low moral standards; contemptible; inferior
11. BEGUILE	Delude; cheat; divert
12. BEMUSED	Confused
13. BLASPHEMY	An irreverent or impious act or utterance
14. CALAMITY	Disaster
15. CALUMNY	False statement maliciously or knowingly made to injure someone
16. CONDEMNATION	Severe reproof; strong censure
17. CONJURED	Summoned by oath or spell
18. CONTEMPLATION	Thoughtful observation or meditation
19. CONTEMPTUOUS	Scornful; distainful
20. CONTENTIOUS	Quarrelsome
21. DAFT	Crazy; foolish; stupid
22. DIABOLISM	Witchcraft; sorcery
23. ECSTATIC	In a state of exalted delight
24. EFFRONTERY	Audacity; insulting boldness
25. EVADE	Escape or avoid by cleverness or deceit
26. FACTION	Small group of people, usually contentious, within a larger group
27. FRAUD	Deliberate deception for unfair or unlawful gain
28. HYPOCRITES	People who say they believe one way but in actious show they believe the opposite
29. INCREDULOUSLY	Disbelievingly
30. INDICTMENT	Statement of criminal charges
31. INDIGNANT	Filled with an anger aroused by something unjust or unworthy
32. INEPTLY	Awkward
33. INERT	Unable to move or act
34. LECHERY	Promiscuity
35. LICENTIOUS	Having no regard for accepted rules or standards
36. MANIFEST	Something apparent to the sight or understanding
37. MENACINGLY	Threateningly
38. PALLOR	Extreme paleness
39. PARTISAN	Militant supporter of a party, cause, faction or idea
40. PENITENCE	Performing of penance
41. PERPLEXED	Bewildered; puzzled; confused
42. PRETENSE	The act of pretending
43. PRODIGIOUS	Extraordinary; marvelous
44. PROPITIATION	Appeasement
45. PROVIDENCE	Work of divine direction
46. QUAIL	To lose courage; decline; fail; give way
47. QUALM	Sensation of misgiving or uneasiness
48. REMORSELESSLY	Mercilessly; having no pity or compassion

The Crucible Vocabulary Word List Continued

No.	Word	Clue/Definition
49.	REPRIEVE	Postponement of punishment
50.	SARCASTICAL	Expressing mocking or contemptuous remarks
51.	STATUTES	Laws, decrees or edicts
52.	TAINTED	Having a moral defect; infected
53.	TRANSFIXED	Rendered motionless with terror, amazement or awe

The Crucible Vocabulary Fill In The Blank 1

1. Something apparent to the sight or understanding
2. Performing of penance
3. Militant supporter of a party, cause, faction or idea
4. Unable to move or act
5. Work of divine direction
6. An irreverent or impious act or utterance
7. Confused
8. Political disorder and confusion
9. Disbelievingly
10. Crazy; foolish; stupid
11. Find out
12. Having low moral standards; contemptible; inferior
13. Enthusiastically
14. Extreme paleness
15. Audacity; insulting boldness
16. Severe reproof; strong censure
17. Bewildered; puzzled; confused
18. To lose courage; decline; fail; give way
19. Extraordinary; marvelous
20. Quarrelsome

The Crucible Vocabulary Fill In The Blank 1 Answer Key

MANIFEST	1. Something apparent to the sight or understanding
PENITENCE	2. Performing of penance
PARTISAN	3. Militant supporter of a party, cause, faction or idea
INERT	4. Unable to move or act
PROVIDENCE	5. Work of divine direction
BLASPHEMY	6. An irreverent or impious act or utterance
BEMUSED	7. Confused
ANARCHY	8. Political disorder and confusion
INCREDULOUSLY	9. Disbelievingly
DAFT	10. Crazy; foolish; stupid
ASCERTAIN	11. Find out
BASE	12. Having low moral standards; contemptible; inferior
AVIDLY	13. Enthusiastically
PALLOR	14. Extreme paleness
EFFRONTERY	15. Audacity; insulting boldness
CONDEMNATION	16. Severe reproof; strong censure
PERPLEXED	17. Bewildered; puzzled; confused
QUAIL	18. To lose courage; decline; fail; give way
PRODIGIOUS	19. Extraordinary; marvelous
CONTENTIOUS	20. Quarrelsome

The Crucible Vocabulary Fil In The Blank 2

_____ 1. Quarrelsome

_____ 2. Having low moral standards; contemptible; inferior

_____ 3. Unable to move or act

_____ 4. Adversaries; opponents

_____ 5. Work of divine direction

_____ 6. Statement of criminal charges

_____ 7. Performing of penance

_____ 8. Severe reproof; strong censure

_____ 9. Crazy; foolish; stupid

_____ 10. The act of pretending

_____ 11. Things that elicit great dislike or abhorrence

_____ 12. Mercilessly; having no pity or compassion

_____ 13. Extraordinary; marvelous

_____ 14. Audacity; insulting boldness

_____ 15. Disbelievingly

_____ 16. People who say they believe one way but in actious show they believe the opposite

_____ 17. False statement maliciously or knowingly made to injure someone

_____ 18. Secrecy; having unknown or unacknowledged name

_____ 19. Having no regard for accepted rules or standards

_____ 20. An irreverent or impious act or utterance

The Crucible Vocabulary Fill In The Blank 2 Answer Key

CONTENTIOUS	1. Quarrelsome
BASE	2. Having low moral standards; contemptible; inferior
INERT	3. Unable to move or act
ANTAGONISTS	4. Adversaries; opponents
PROVIDENCE	5. Work of divine direction
INDICTMENT	6. Statement of criminal charges
PENITENCE	7. Performing of penance
CONDEMNATION	8. Severe reproof; strong censure
DAFT	9. Crazy; foolish; stupid
PRETENSE	10. The act of pretending
ABOMINATIONS	11. Things that elicit great dislike or abhorrence
REMORSELESSLY	12. Mercilessly; having no pity or compassion
PRODIGIOUS	13. Extraordinary; marvelous
EFFRONTERY	14. Audacity; insulting boldness
INCREDULOUSLY	15. Disbelievingly
HYPOCRITES	16. People who say they believe one way but in actious show they believe the opposite
CALUMNY	17. False statement maliciously or knowingly made to injure someone
ANONYMITY	18. Secrecy; having unknown or unacknowledged name
LICENTIOUS	19. Having no regard for accepted rules or standards
BLASPHEMY	20. An irreverent or impious act or utterance

The Crucible Vocabulary Fill In The Blank 3

_____ 1. Bewildered; puzzled; confused

_____ 2. To lose courage; decline; fail; give way

_____ 3. Witchcraft; sorcery

_____ 4. Appeasement

_____ 5. Secrecy; having unknown or unacknowledged name

_____ 6. Severe reproof; strong censure

_____ 7. Extreme paleness

_____ 8. Summoned by oath or spell

_____ 9. Able to be heard

_____ 10. The act of pretending

_____ 11. Disaster

_____ 12. Extraordinary; marvelous

_____ 13. Thoughtful observation or meditation

_____ 14. Delude; cheat; divert

_____ 15. Quarrelsome

_____ 16. Something apparent to the sight or understanding

_____ 17. Confused

_____ 18. False statement maliciously or knowingly made to injure someone

_____ 19. Mercilessly; having no pity or compassion

_____ 20. Having no regard for accepted rules or standards

The Crucible Vocabulary Fill In The Blank 3 Answer Key

PERPLEXED	1. Bewildered; puzzled; confused
QUAIL	2. To lose courage; decline; fail; give way
DIABOLISM	3. Witchcraft; sorcery
PROPITIATION	4. Appeasement
ANONYMITY	5. Secrecy; having unknown or unacknowledged name
CONDEMNATION	6. Severe reproof; strong censure
PALLOR	7. Extreme paleness
CONJURED	8. Summoned by oath or spell
AUDIBLE	9. Able to be heard
PRETENSE	10. The act of pretending
CALAMITY	11. Disaster
PRODIGIOUS	12. Extraordinary; marvelous
CONTEMPLATION	13. Thoughtful observation or meditation
BEGUILE	14. Delude; cheat; divert
CONTENTIOUS	15. Quarrelsome
MANIFEST	16. Something apparent to the sight or understanding
BEMUSED	17. Confused
CALUMNY	18. False statement maliciously or knowingly made to injure someone
REMORSELESSLY	19. Mercilessly; having no pity or compassion
LICENTIOUS	20. Having no regard for accepted rules or standards

The Crucible Vocabulary Fill In The Blank 4

1. Sensation of misgiving or uneasiness
2. Laws, decrees or edicts
3. To lose courage; decline; fail; give way
4. Mercilessly; having no pity or compassion
5. Awkward
6. Witchcraft; sorcery
7. Performing of penance
8. Promiscuity
9. Loyalty
10. Find out
11. Secrecy; having unknown or unacknowledged name
12. Adversaries; opponents
13. Escape or avoid by cleverness or deceit
14. Thoughtful observation or meditation
15. Deliberate deception for unfair or unlawful gain
16. Delude; cheat; divert
17. Work of divine direction
18. Militant supporter of a party, cause, faction or idea
19. Summoned by oath or spell
20. Rendered motionless with terror, amazement or awe

The Crucible Vocabulary Fill In The Blank 4 Answer Key

QUALM	1. Sensation of misgiving or uneasiness
STATUTES	2. Laws, decrees or edicts
QUAIL	3. To lose courage; decline; fail; give way
REMORSELESSLY	4. Mercilessly; having no pity or compassion
INEPTLY	5. Awkward
DIABOLISM	6. Witchcraft; sorcery
PENITENCE	7. Performing of penance
LECHERY	8. Promiscuity
ALLEGIANCE	9. Loyalty
ASCERTAIN	10. Find out
ANONYMITY	11. Secrecy; having unknown or unacknowledged name
ANTAGONISTS	12. Adversaries; opponents
EVADE	13. Escape or avoid by cleverness or deceit
CONTEMPLATION	14. Thoughtful observation or meditation
FRAUD	15. Deliberate deception for unfair or unlawful gain
BEGUILE	16. Delude; cheat; divert
PROVIDENCE	17. Work of divine direction
PARTISAN	18. Militant supporter of a party, cause, faction or idea
CONJURED	19. Summoned by oath or spell
TRANSFIXED	20. Rendered motionless with terror, amazement or awe

The Crucible Vocabulary Matching 1

___ 1. BEGUILE   A. Audacity; insulting boldness
___ 2. QUALM   B. Awkward
___ 3. DIABOLISM   C. Escape or avoid by cleverness or deceit
___ 4. ALLEGIANCE   D. The act of pretending
___ 5. PRETENSE   E. Able to be heard
___ 6. BEMUSED   F. Mercilessly; having no pity or compassion
___ 7. EFFRONTERY   G. People who say they believe one way but in actious show they believe the opposite
___ 8. CONDEMNATION   H. Promiscuity
___ 9. DAFT   I. Witchcraft; sorcery
___10. REMORSELESSLY   J. Confused
___11. INEPTLY   K. Appeasement
___12. SARCASTICAL   L. Firm in purpose or opinion; unyielding
___13. INCREDULOUSLY   M. Things that elicit great dislike or abhorrence
___14. FRAUD   N. Loyalty
___15. ABOMINATIONS   O. Postponement of punishment
___16. LECHERY   P. Sensation of misgiving or uneasiness
___17. ECSTATIC   Q. Threateningly
___18. EVADE   R. In a state of exalted delight
___19. PROPITIATION   S. Disbelievingly
___20. ADAMANT   T. Deliberate deception for unfair or unlawful gain
___21. MENACINGLY   U. Severe reproof; strong censure
___22. HYPOCRITES   V. Delude; cheat; divert
___23. ANARCHY   W. Expressing mocking or contemptuous remarks
___24. REPRIEVE   X. Crazy; foolish; stupid
___25. AUDIBLE   Y. Political disorder and confusion

The Crucible Vocabulary Matching 1 Answer Key

V - 1. BEGUILE		A. Audacity; insulting boldness
P - 2. QUALM		B. Awkward
I - 3. DIABOLISM		C. Escape or avoid by cleverness or deceit
N - 4. ALLEGIANCE		D. The act of pretending
D - 5. PRETENSE		E. Able to be heard
J - 6. BEMUSED		F. Mercilessly; having no pity or compassion
A - 7. EFFRONTERY		G. People who say they believe one way but in actious show they believe the opposite
U - 8. CONDEMNATION		H. Promiscuity
X - 9. DAFT		I. Witchcraft; sorcery
F - 10. REMORSELESSLY		J. Confused
B - 11. INEPTLY		K. Appeasement
W - 12. SARCASTICAL		L. Firm in purpose or opinion; unyielding
S - 13. INCREDULOUSLY		M. Things that elicit great dislike or abhorrence
T - 14. FRAUD		N. Loyalty
M - 15. ABOMINATIONS		O. Postponement of punishment
H - 16. LECHERY		P. Sensation of misgiving or uneasiness
R - 17. ECSTATIC		Q. Threateningly
C - 18. EVADE		R. In a state of exalted delight
K - 19. PROPITIATION		S. Disbelievingly
L - 20. ADAMANT		T. Deliberate deception for unfair or unlawful gain
Q - 21. MENACINGLY		U. Severe reproof; strong censure
G - 22. HYPOCRITES		V. Delude; cheat; divert
Y - 23. ANARCHY		W. Expressing mocking or contemptuous remarks
O - 24. REPRIEVE		X. Crazy; foolish; stupid
E - 25. AUDIBLE		Y. Political disorder and confusion

The Crucible Vocabulary Matching 2

___ 1. REMORSELESSLY   A. Find out
___ 2. INDICTMENT   B. Mercilessly; having no pity or compassion
___ 3. ANONYMITY   C. Thoughtful observation or meditation
___ 4. CALUMNY   D. Summoned by oath or spell
___ 5. BEMUSED   E. Postponement of punishment
___ 6. TRANSFIXED   F. Unable to move or act
___ 7. BLASPHEMY   G. Witchcraft; sorcery
___ 8. EFFRONTERY   H. Enthusiastically
___ 9. LECHERY   I. Secrecy; having unknown or unacknowledged name
___ 10. QUAIL   J. Statement of criminal charges
___ 11. FRAUD   K. Able to be heard
___ 12. CONJURED   L. Political disorder and confusion
___ 13. ANARCHY   M. Audacity; insulting boldness
___ 14. INERT   N. Confused
___ 15. DIABOLISM   O. Promiscuity
___ 16. INEPTLY   P. Escape or avoid by cleverness or deceit
___ 17. ASCERTAIN   Q. An irreverent or impious act or utterance
___ 18. AVIDLY   R. Loyalty
___ 19. EVADE   S. Rendered motionless with terror, amazement or awe
___ 20. REPRIEVE   T. Firm in purpose or opinion; unyielding
___ 21. PRODIGIOUS   U. Awkward
___ 22. CONTEMPLATION   V. Extraordinary; marvelous
___ 23. ADAMANT   W. False statement maliciously or knowingly made to injure someone
___ 24. AUDIBLE   X. Deliberate deception for unfair or unlawful gain
___ 25. ALLEGIANCE   Y. To lose courage; decline; fail; give way

The Crucible Vocabulary Matching 2 Answer Key

B - 1.	REMORSELESSLY	A.	Find out
J - 2.	INDICTMENT	B.	Mercilessly; having no pity or compassion
I - 3.	ANONYMITY	C.	Thoughtful observation or meditation
W - 4.	CALUMNY	D.	Summoned by oath or spell
N - 5.	BEMUSED	E.	Postponement of punishment
S - 6.	TRANSFIXED	F.	Unable to move or act
Q - 7.	BLASPHEMY	G.	Witchcraft; sorcery
M - 8.	EFFRONTERY	H.	Enthusiastically
O - 9.	LECHERY	I.	Secrecy; having unknown or unacknowledged name
Y - 10.	QUAIL	J.	Statement of criminal charges
X - 11.	FRAUD	K.	Able to be heard
D - 12.	CONJURED	L.	Political disorder and confusion
L - 13.	ANARCHY	M.	Audacity; insulting boldness
F - 14.	INERT	N.	Confused
G - 15.	DIABOLISM	O.	Promiscuity
U - 16.	INEPTLY	P.	Escape or avoid by cleverness or deceit
A - 17.	ASCERTAIN	Q.	An irreverent or impious act or utterance
H - 18.	AVIDLY	R.	Loyalty
P - 19.	EVADE	S.	Rendered motionless with terror, amazement or awe
E - 20.	REPRIEVE	T.	Firm in purpose or opinion; unyielding
V - 21.	PRODIGIOUS	U.	Awkward
C - 22.	CONTEMPLATION	V.	Extraordinary; marvelous
T - 23.	ADAMANT	W.	False statement maliciously or knowingly made to injure someone
K - 24.	AUDIBLE	X.	Deliberate deception for unfair or unlawful gain
R - 25.	ALLEGIANCE	Y.	To lose courage; decline; fail; give way

The Crucible Vocabulary Matching 3

___ 1. PALLOR
___ 2. CONDEMNATION
___ 3. REPRIEVE
___ 4. MENACINGLY
___ 5. ALLEGIANCE
___ 6. BEGUILE
___ 7. PARTISAN
___ 8. ANARCHY
___ 9. INCREDULOUSLY
___ 10. LICENTIOUS
___ 11. PROVIDENCE
___ 12. CONJURED
___ 13. FRAUD
___ 14. FACTION
___ 15. BASE
___ 16. PERPLEXED
___ 17. INEPTLY
___ 18. BEMUSED
___ 19. EFFRONTERY
___ 20. QUAIL
___ 21. ECSTATIC
___ 22. STATUTES
___ 23. PRETENSE
___ 24. TRANSFIXED
___ 25. EVADE

A. The act of pretending
B. Postponement of punishment
C. Small group of people, usually contentious, within a larger group
D. Severe reproof; strong censure
E. Threateningly
F. Audacity; insulting boldness
G. To lose courage; decline; fail; give way
H. Bewildered; puzzled; confused
I. Deliberate deception for unfair or unlawful gain
J. Loyalty
K. Political disorder and confusion
L. Escape or avoid by cleverness or deceit
M. Disbelievingly
N. Militant supporter of a party, cause, faction or idea
O. Extreme paleness
P. Having low moral standards; contemptible; inferior
Q. Having no regard for accepted rules or standards
R. Confused
S. Rendered motionless with terror, amazement or awe
T. Delude; cheat; divert
U. Work of divine direction
V. Awkward
W. Summoned by oath or spell
X. In a state of exalted delight
Y. Laws, decrees or edicts

The Crucible Vocabulary Matching 3 Answer Key

O - 1.	PALLOR	A.	The act of pretending
D - 2.	CONDEMNATION	B.	Postponement of punishment
B - 3.	REPRIEVE	C.	Small group of people, usually contentious, within a larger group
E - 4.	MENACINGLY	D.	Severe reproof; strong censure
J - 5.	ALLEGIANCE	E.	Threateningly
T - 6.	BEGUILE	F.	Audacity; insulting boldness
N - 7.	PARTISAN	G.	To lose courage; decline; fail; give way
K - 8.	ANARCHY	H.	Bewildered; puzzled; confused
M - 9.	INCREDULOUSLY	I.	Deliberate deception for unfair or unlawful gain
Q -10.	LICENTIOUS	J.	Loyalty
U -11.	PROVIDENCE	K.	Political disorder and confusion
W -12.	CONJURED	L.	Escape or avoid by cleverness or deceit
I - 13.	FRAUD	M.	Disbelievingly
C -14.	FACTION	N.	Militant supporter of a party, cause, faction or idea
P -15.	BASE	O.	Extreme paleness
H -16.	PERPLEXED	P.	Having low moral standards; contemptible; inferior
V -17.	INEPTLY	Q.	Having no regard for accepted rules or standards
R -18.	BEMUSED	R.	Confused
F -19.	EFFRONTERY	S.	Rendered motionless with terror, amazement or awe
G -20.	QUAIL	T.	Delude; cheat; divert
X -21.	ECSTATIC	U.	Work of divine direction
Y -22.	STATUTES	V.	Awkward
A -23.	PRETENSE	W.	Summoned by oath or spell
S -24.	TRANSFIXED	X.	In a state of exalted delight
L -25.	EVADE	Y.	Laws, decrees or edicts

The Crucible Vocabulary Matching 4

___ 1. CONJURED
___ 2. PERPLEXED
___ 3. PROPITIATION
___ 4. INEPTLY
___ 5. ASCERTAIN
___ 6. ABOMINATIONS
___ 7. ECSTATIC
___ 8. TRANSFIXED
___ 9. PRODIGIOUS
___ 10. PARTISAN
___ 11. REPRIEVE
___ 12. BEGUILE
___ 13. BLASPHEMY
___ 14. CONDEMNATION
___ 15. STATUTES
___ 16. PALLOR
___ 17. CALUMNY
___ 18. DIABOLISM
___ 19. QUALM
___ 20. INCREDULOUSLY
___ 21. PROVIDENCE
___ 22. BASE
___ 23. CONTEMPLATION
___ 24. EVADE
___ 25. PENITENCE

A. Awkward
B. Thoughtful observation or meditation
C. An irreverent or impious act or utterance
D. Performing of penance
E. Postponement of punishment
F. Things that elicit great dislike or abhorrence
G. In a state of exalted delight
H. Extreme paleness
I. Severe reproof; strong censure
J. Extraordinary; marvelous
K. Witchcraft; sorcery
L. Delude; cheat; divert
M. Rendered motionless with terror, amazement or awe
N. Disbelievingly
O. Appeasement
P. Work of divine direction
Q. Summoned by oath or spell
R. Escape or avoid by cleverness or deceit
S. Bewildered; puzzled; confused
T. Having low moral standards; contemptible; inferior
U. Militant supporter of a party, cause, faction or idea
V. Find out
W. False statement maliciously or knowingly made to injure someone
X. Laws, decrees or edicts
Y. Sensation of misgiving or uneasiness

The Crucible Vocabulary Matching 4 Answer Key

Q - 1. CONJURED	A.	Awkward
S - 2. PERPLEXED	B.	Thoughtful observation or meditation
O - 3. PROPITIATION	C.	An irreverent or impious act or utterance
A - 4. INEPTLY	D.	Performing of penance
V - 5. ASCERTAIN	E.	Postponement of punishment
F - 6. ABOMINATIONS	F.	Things that elicit great dislike or abhorrence
G - 7. ECSTATIC	G.	In a state of exalted delight
M - 8. TRANSFIXED	H.	Extreme paleness
J - 9. PRODIGIOUS	I.	Severe reproof; strong censure
U -10. PARTISAN	J.	Extraordinary; marvelous
E -11. REPRIEVE	K.	Witchcraft; sorcery
L -12. BEGUILE	L.	Delude; cheat; divert
C -13. BLASPHEMY	M.	Rendered motionless with terror, amazement or awe
I -14. CONDEMNATION	N.	Disbelievingly
X -15. STATUTES	O.	Appeasement
H -16. PALLOR	P.	Work of divine direction
W -17. CALUMNY	Q.	Summoned by oath or spell
K -18. DIABOLISM	R.	Escape or avoid by cleverness or deceit
Y -19. QUALM	S.	Bewildered; puzzled; confused
N -20. INCREDULOUSLY	T.	Having low moral standards; contemptible; inferior
P -21. PROVIDENCE	U.	Militant supporter of a party, cause, faction or idea
T -22. BASE	V.	Find out
B -23. CONTEMPLATION	W.	False statement maliciously or knowingly made to injure someone
R -24. EVADE	X.	Laws, decrees or edicts
D -25. PENITENCE	Y.	Sensation of misgiving or uneasiness

The Crucible Vocabulary Magic Squares 1

Match the definition with the vocabulary word. Put your answers in the magic squares below. When your answers are correct, all columns and rows will add to the same number.

A. HYPOCRITES
B. ADAMANT
C. PARTISAN
D. CALAMITY
E. TAINTED
F. LICENTIOUS
G. CONTENTIOUS
H. AUDIBLE
I. AVIDLY
J. EFFRONTERY
K. CONTEMPTUOUS
L. BLASPHEMY
M. ASCERTAIN
N. ANONYMITY
O. DAFT
P. ECSTATIC

1. People who say they believe one way but in actious show they believe the opposite
2. Secrecy; having unknown or unacknowledged name
3. Audacity; insulting boldness
4. Having a moral defect; infected
5. Quarrelsome
6. An irreverent or impious act or utterance
7. In a state of exalted delight
8. Militant supporter of a party, cause, faction or idea
9. Crazy; foolish; stupid
10. Disaster
11. Able to be heard
12. Scornful; distainful
13. Enthusiastically
14. Having no regard for accepted rules or standards
15. Firm in purpose or opinion; unyielding
16. Find out

A=	B=	C=	D=
E=	F=	G=	H=
I=	J=	K=	L=
M=	N=	O=	P=

The Crucible Vocabulary Magic Squares 1 Answer Key

Match the definition with the vocabulary word. Put your answers in the magic squares below. When your answers are correct, all columns and rows will add to the same number.

A. HYPOCRITES
B. ADAMANT
C. PARTISAN
D. CALAMITY
E. TAINTED
F. LICENTIOUS
G. CONTENTIOUS
H. AUDIBLE
I. AVIDLY
J. EFFRONTERY
K. CONTEMPTUOUS
L. BLASPHEMY
M. ASCERTAIN
N. ANONYMITY
O. DAFT
P. ECSTATIC

1. People who say they believe one way but in actious show they believe the opposite
2. Secrecy; having unknown or unacknowledged name
3. Audacity; insulting boldness
4. Having a moral defect; infected
5. Quarrelsome
6. An irreverent or impious act or utterance
7. In a state of exalted delight
8. Militant supporter of a party, cause, faction or idea
9. Crazy; foolish; stupid
10. Disaster
11. Able to be heard
12. Scornful; distainful
13. Enthusiastically
14. Having no regard for accepted rules or standards
15. Firm in purpose or opinion; unyielding
16. Find out

A=1	B=15	C=8	D=10
E=4	F=14	G=5	H=11
I=13	J=3	K=12	L=6
M=16	N=2	O=9	P=7

The Crucible Vocabulary Magic Squares 2

A. LICENTIOUS
B. ECSTATIC
C. ANTAGONISTS
D. CONTEMPTUOUS
E. EVADE
F. ABOMINATIONS
G. AUDIBLE
H. ASCERTAIN
I. CALAMITY
J. PROPITIATION
K. TRANSFIXED
L. PROVIDENCE
M. CALUMNY
N. FACTION
O. ADAMANT
P. AVIDLY

1. Find out
2. Having no regard for accepted rules or standards
3. In a state of exalted delight
4. Able to be heard
5. Appeasement
6. Firm in purpose or opinion; unyielding
7. Enthusiastically
8. Disaster
9. Rendered motionless with terror, amazement or awe
10. Small group of people, usually contentious, within a larger group
11. False statement maliciously or knowingly made to injure someone
12. Work of divine direction
13. Escape or avoid by cleverness or deceit
14. Scornful; distainful
15. Adversaries; opponents
16. Things that elicit great dislike or abhorrence

A=	B=	C=	D=
E=	F=	G=	H=
I=	J=	K=	L=
M=	N=	O=	P=

The Crucible Vocabulary Magic Squares 2 Answer Key

A. LICENTIOUS
B. ECSTATIC
C. ANTAGONISTS
D. CONTEMPTUOUS
E. EVADE
F. ABOMINATIONS
G. AUDIBLE
H. ASCERTAIN
I. CALAMITY
J. PROPITIATION
K. TRANSFIXED
L. PROVIDENCE
M. CALUMNY
N. FACTION
O. ADAMANT
P. AVIDLY

1. Find out
2. Having no regard for accepted rules or standards
3. In a state of exalted delight
4. Able to be heard
5. Appeasement
6. Firm in purpose or opinion; unyielding
7. Enthusiastically
8. Disaster
9. Rendered motionless with terror, amazement or awe
10. Small group of people, usually contentious, within a larger group
11. False statement maliciously or knowingly made to injure someone
12. Work of divine direction
13. Escape or avoid by cleverness or deceit
14. Scornful; distainful
15. Adversaries; opponents
16. Things that elicit great dislike or abhorrence

A=2	B=3	C=15	D=14
E=13	F=16	G=4	H=1
I=8	J=5	K=9	L=12
M=11	N=10	O=6	P=7

The Crucible Vocabulary Magic Squares 3

Match the definition with the vocabulary word. Put your answers in the magic squares below. When your answers are correct, all columns and rows will add to the same number.

A. BEMUSED
B. DAFT
C. PERPLEXED
D. ALLEGIANCE
E. CONDEMNATION
F. LECHERY
G. INDICTMENT
H. FRAUD
I. TAINTED
J. EVADE
K. ADAMANT
L. CONTENTIOUS
M. SARCASTICAL
N. PROVIDENCE
O. CONJURED
P. AVIDLY

1. Summoned by oath or spell
2. Escape or avoid by cleverness or deceit
3. Deliberate deception for unfair or unlawful gain
4. Confused
5. Loyalty
6. Severe reproof; strong censure
7. Firm in purpose or opinion; unyielding
8. Work of divine direction
9. Promiscuity
10. Bewildered; puzzled; confused
11. Expressing mocking or contemptuous remarks
12. Quarrelsome
13. Having a moral defect; infected
14. Enthusiastically
15. Crazy; foolish; stupid
16. Statement of criminal charges

A=	B=	C=	D=
E=	F=	G=	H=
I=	J=	K=	L=
M=	N=	O=	P=

The Crucible Vocabulary Magic Squares 3 Answer Key

Match the definition with the vocabulary word. Put your answers in the magic squares below. When your answers are correct, all columns and rows will add to the same number.

A. BEMUSED
B. DAFT
C. PERPLEXED
D. ALLEGIANCE
E. CONDEMNATION
F. LECHERY
G. INDICTMENT
H. FRAUD
I. TAINTED
J. EVADE
K. ADAMANT
L. CONTENTIOUS
M. SARCASTICAL
N. PROVIDENCE
O. CONJURED
P. AVIDLY

1. Summoned by oath or spell
2. Escape or avoid by cleverness or deceit
3. Deliberate deception for unfair or unlawful gain
4. Confused
5. Loyalty
6. Severe reproof; strong censure
7. Firm in purpose or opinion; unyielding
8. Work of divine direction
9. Promiscuity
10. Bewildered; puzzled; confused
11. Expressing mocking or contemptuous remarks
12. Quarrelsome
13. Having a moral defect; infected
14. Enthusiastically
15. Crazy; foolish; stupid
16. Statement of criminal charges

A=4	B=15	C=10	D=5
E=6	F=9	G=16	H=3
I=13	J=2	K=7	L=12
M=11	N=8	O=1	P=14

The Crucible Vocabulary Magic Squares 4

Match the definition with the vocabulary word. Put your answers in the magic squares below. When your answers are correct, all columns and rows will add to the same number.

A. DIABOLISM
B. ALLEGIANCE
C. CALAMITY
D. CONDEMNATION
E. CONTEMPLATION
F. QUALM
G. DAFT
H. SARCASTICAL
I. PENITENCE
J. EVADE
K. STATUTES
L. CONTEMPTUOUS
M. ANTAGONISTS
N. ANARCHY
O. BEMUSED
P. LECHERY

1. Confused
2. Severe reproof; strong censure
3. Escape or avoid by cleverness or deceit
4. Thoughtful observation or meditation
5. Performing of penance
6. Sensation of misgiving or uneasiness
7. Promiscuity
8. Disaster
9. Expressing mocking or contemptuous remarks
10. Laws, decrees or edicts
11. Witchcraft; sorcery
12. Political disorder and confusion
13. Loyalty
14. Adversaries; opponents
15. Crazy; foolish; stupid
16. Scornful; distainful

A=	B=	C=	D=
E=	F=	G=	H=
I=	J=	K=	L=
M=	N=	O=	P=

The Crucible Vocabulary Magic Squares 4 Answer Key

Match the definition with the vocabulary word. Put your answers in the magic squares below. When your answers are correct, all columns and rows will add to the same number.

A. DIABOLISM
B. ALLEGIANCE
C. CALAMITY
D. CONDEMNATION
E. CONTEMPLATION
F. QUALM
G. DAFT
H. SARCASTICAL
I. PENITENCE
J. EVADE
K. STATUTES
L. CONTEMPTUOUS
M. ANTAGONISTS
N. ANARCHY
O. BEMUSED
P. LECHERY

1. Confused
2. Severe reproof; strong censure
3. Escape or avoid by cleverness or deceit
4. Thoughtful observation or meditation
5. Performing of penance
6. Sensation of misgiving or uneasiness
7. Promiscuity
8. Disaster
9. Expressing mocking or contemptuous remarks
10. Laws, decrees or edicts
11. Witchcraft; sorcery
12. Political disorder and confusion
13. Loyalty
14. Adversaries; opponents
15. Crazy; foolish; stupid
16. Scornful; distainful

A=11	B=13	C=8	D=2
E=4	F=6	G=15	H=9
I=5	J=3	K=10	L=16
M=14	N=12	O=1	P=7

The Crucible Vocabulary Word Search 1

```
L S Z E Q R V H T C A V I D L Y A E M S
F T S G L P B N F H A T Z C I F N C E N
V A T P X E A N A V S L E T A N A S N S
B N C Y R N C T D U C C U Q U J R T A G
L L D T G O R H O N N O A M Q B C A C P
T T A I I E P I E E X N X L N H H T I Z
R R D S N O T I D R G T D I A Y Y I N H
E N A I P N N I T E Y E A C N M P C G R
I F P N E H V N V I T M B E F E I C L C
P S F T S O E E F N A P O N R L P T Y G
F A N R R F I M I D P T M T A B I T Y D
P O L P O R I A Y E R U I I U I N D L Q
C E B L P N T X S V O O N O D D D I M Y
B Q N E O Z T N E A D U A U N U I A A N
E U R I R R E E Y D I S T S G A C B N W
M A D R T T Q S R E G F I X Y Z T O I M
U L H H E E H R K Y I W O P T Y M L F W
S M Y R G G N M L L O L N W L Y E I E R
E Q P H M H C C P M U P S F H Q N S S K
D M V N I A T R E C S A M G F R T M T P
```

Able to be heard (7)
An irreverent or impious act or utterance (9)
Appeasement (12)
Audacity; insulting boldness (10)
Awkward (7)
Confused (7)
Crazy; foolish; stupid (4)
Deliberate deception for unfair or unlawful gain (5)
Disaster (8)
Enthusiastically (6)
Escape or avoid by cleverness or deceit (5)
Extraordinary; marvelous (10)
Extreme paleness (6)
False statement maliciously or knowingly made to injure someone (7)
Filled with an anger aroused by something unjust or unworthy (9)
Find out (9)
Having a moral defect; infected (7)
Having low moral standards; contemptible; inferior (4)
Having no regard for accepted rules or standards (10)
In a state of exalted delight (8)
Performing of penance (9)

Political disorder and confusion (7)
Postponement of punishment (8)
Promiscuity (7)
Quarrelsome (11)
Rendered motionless with terror, amazement or awe (10)
Scornful; distainful (12)
Sensation of misgiving or uneasiness (5)
Small group of people, usually contentious, within a larger group (7)
Something apparent to the sight or understanding (8)
Statement of criminal charges (10)
The act of pretending (8)
Things that elicit great dislike or abhorrence (12)
Threateningly (10)
To lose courage; decline; fail; give way (5)
Unable to move or act (5)
Witchcraft; sorcery (9)
Work of divine direction (10)

The Crucible Vocabulary Word Search 1 Answer Key

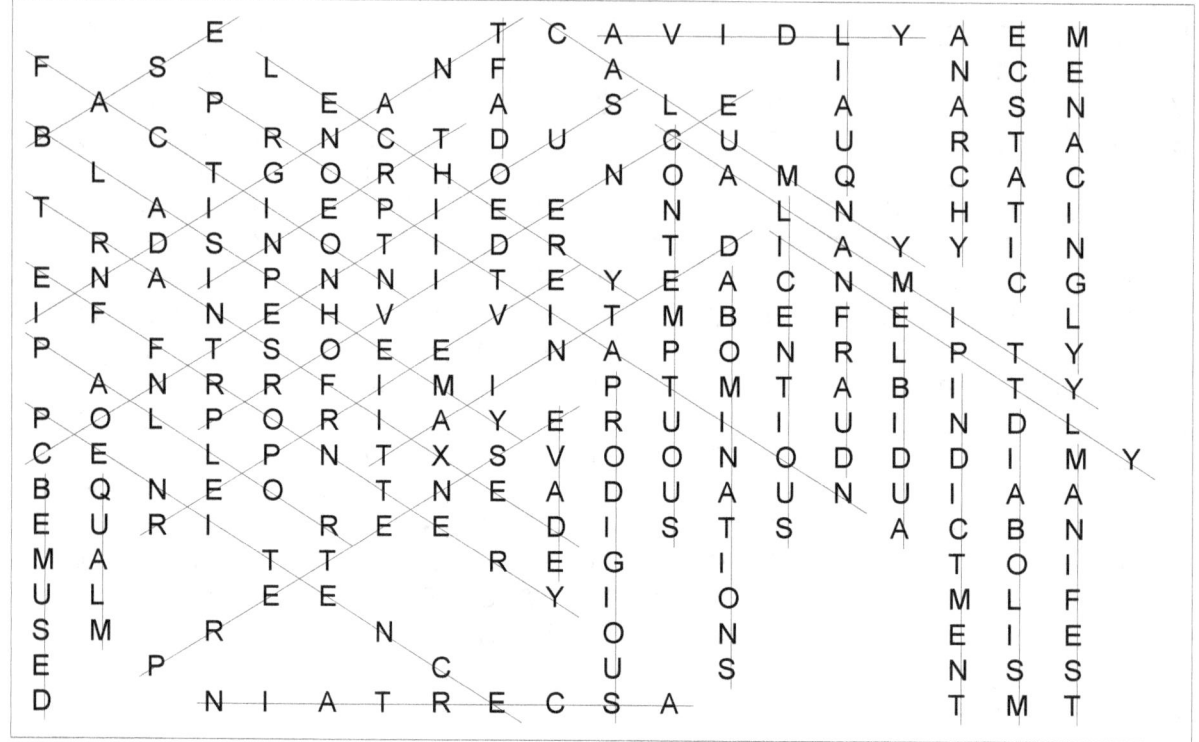

Able to be heard (7)
An irreverent or impious act or utterance (9)
Appeasement (12)
Audacity; insulting boldness (10)
Awkward (7)
Confused (7)
Crazy; foolish; stupid (4)
Deliberate deception for unfair or unlawful gain (5)
Disaster (8)
Enthusiastically (6)
Escape or avoid by cleverness or deceit (5)
Extraordinary; marvelous (10)
Extreme paleness (6)
False statement maliciously or knowingly made to injure someone (7)
Filled with an anger aroused by something unjust or unworthy (9)
Find out (9)
Having a moral defect; infected (7)
Having low moral standards; contemptible; inferior (4)
Having no regard for accepted rules or standards (10)
In a state of exalted delight (8)
Performing of penance (9)

Political disorder and confusion (7)
Postponement of punishment (8)
Promiscuity (7)
Quarrelsome (11)
Rendered motionless with terror, amazement or awe (10)
Scornful; distainful (12)
Sensation of misgiving or uneasiness (5)
Small group of people, usually contentious, within a larger group (7)
Something apparent to the sight or understanding (8)
Statement of criminal charges (10)
The act of pretending (8)
Things that elicit great dislike or abhorrence (12)
Threateningly (10)
To lose courage; decline; fail; give way (5)
Unable to move or act (5)
Witchcraft; sorcery (9)
Work of divine direction (10)

The Crucible Vocabulary Word Search 2

```
R D E R U J N O C E A N O N Y M I T Y P
R E P R I E V E A S M A N I F E S T T P
N P M V F D Y G L N T B G P L T Q Y A F
D E L O S H L G U E Q I D C A R L L M X
E R D E R Y Z P M T N U N I L S L Q S Z
L P L K C S B H N E A W N E U O T L I Y
B L A S P H E M Y R E T N O R F F E L Q
I E H S S L E L F P E K L P A T C D O G
D X D J I Y T R E D O U N D J N I A B N
U E B U N P N B Y S D C T Z E V Q V A C
A D G A E W R C U E S N R D A T U E I G
X E K N S X L O R B A L I I N G A C D L
B C I B K E I C D N E V Y E T L I N A M
H Z H K S T N H G I O M M N V E L E D S
C J S Y N I Q I W R G T U C P Q S T A L
K X G E N N D U P B C I Y S M Q X I M B
Y H C R A N A Z A I H Z O V E Y D N A V
M I F W I L V F D L L W T U Y D Y E N V
L F A C T I O N M Z M T Y D S N G P T P
E C S T A T I C A B O M I N A T I O N S
```

Able to be heard (7)
An irreverent or impious act or utterance (9)
Audacity; insulting boldness (10)
Awkward (7)
Bewildered; puzzled; confused (9)
Confused (7)
Crazy; foolish; stupid (4)
Deliberate deception for unfair or unlawful gain (5)
Delude; cheat; divert (7)
Disbelievingly (13)
Enthusiastically (6)
Escape or avoid by cleverness or deceit (5)
Extraordinary; marvelous (10)
Extreme paleness (6)
False statement maliciously or knowingly made to injure someone (7)
Filled with an anger aroused by something unjust or unworthy (9)
Firm in purpose or opinion; unyielding (7)
Having a moral defect; infected (7)
Having low moral standards; contemptible; inferior (4)
Having no regard for accepted rules or standards (10)
In a state of exalted delight (8)

Mercilessly; having no pity or compassion (13)
People who say they believe one way but in actious show they believe the opposite (10)
Performing of penance (9)
Political disorder and confusion (7)
Postponement of punishment (8)
Promiscuity (7)
Secrecy; having unknown or unacknowledged name (9)
Sensation of misgiving or uneasiness (5)
Small group of people, usually contentious, within a larger group (7)
Something apparent to the sight or understanding (8)
Statement of criminal charges (10)
Summoned by oath or spell (8)
The act of pretending (8)
Things that elicit great dislike or abhorrence (12)
To lose courage; decline; fail; give way (5)
Unable to move or act (5)
Witchcraft; sorcery (9)
Work of divine direction (10)

The Crucible Vocabulary Word Search 2 Answer Key

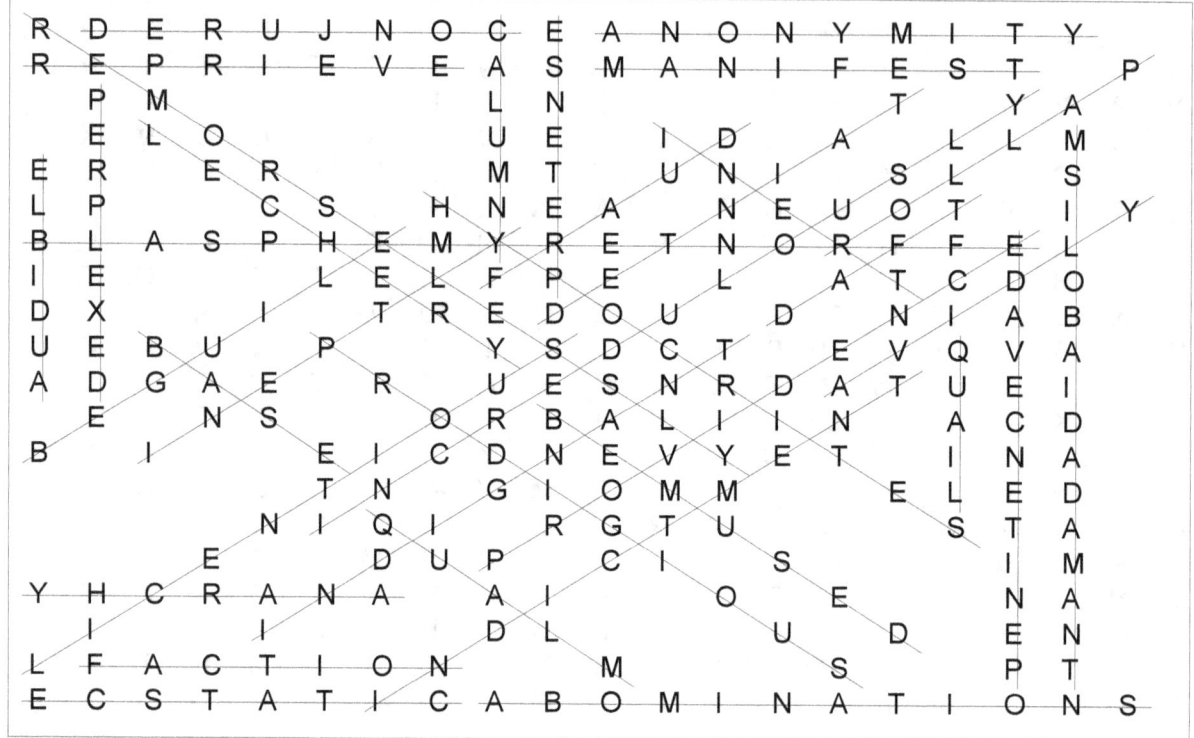

Able to be heard (7)
An irreverent or impious act or utterance (9)
Audacity; insulting boldness (10)
Awkward (7)
Bewildered; puzzled; confused (9)
Confused (7)
Crazy; foolish; stupid (4)
Deliberate deception for unfair or unlawful gain (5)
Delude; cheat; divert (7)
Disbelievingly (13)
Enthusiastically (6)
Escape or avoid by cleverness or deceit (5)
Extraordinary; marvelous (10)
Extreme paleness (6)
False statement maliciously or knowingly made to injure someone (7)
Filled with an anger aroused by something unjust or unworthy (9)
Firm in purpose or opinion; unyielding (7)
Having a moral defect; infected (7)
Having low moral standards; contemptible; inferior (4)
Having no regard for accepted rules or standards (10)
In a state of exalted delight (8)

Mercilessly; having no pity or compassion (13)
People who say they believe one way but in actious show they believe the opposite (10)
Performing of penance (9)
Political disorder and confusion (7)
Postponement of punishment (8)
Promiscuity (7)
Secrecy; having unknown or unacknowledged name (9)
Sensation of misgiving or uneasiness (5)
Small group of people, usually contentious, within a larger group (7)
Something apparent to the sight or understanding (8)
Statement of criminal charges (10)
Summoned by oath or spell (8)
The act of pretending (8)
Things that elicit great dislike or abhorrence (12)
To lose courage; decline; fail; give way (5)
Unable to move or act (5)
Witchcraft; sorcery (9)
Work of divine direction (10)

The Crucible Vocabulary Word Search 3

```
A W Q C Z W G V Q I A H G D F L Q C I C
U V Y G D E X I F S N A R T R F U A N S
D F G X Q A Z M X I T D B L A X A L E V
I F P L C P F G A X A E I E U L L A P T
B E M U S E D T K S G F A C D K M M T B
L A J M R W R D K U O T B H T G Q I L Z
E T S J T E M S I L N B O E Q M P T Y F
I L K E C C P L T A I D M R X J E Y L J
N Y S S V Q E R M A S T I Y Y V N N R F
C R A Y D A Y A I N T T N R Y Y I P T J
R E R N N I D W K E S U A T Y J T A M G
E T C G A A A E Y E V H T H I N E R T B
D N A S H R B B F B C E I E E S N T C K
U O S Q T N C I O O L Y O S S F C I O B
L R T M H A N H N L N A N L X Z E S N Q
O F I L E A T T Y M I E S Y Q S L A T D
U F C N M N E I U Q T S T P E H K N E F
S E A W D N A L C E U I M T H D C X M V
L S L P T I A C R S M A I F E E E H P Q
Y H R I A C G P I Y M R I R A L M J L P
T V O K I L P N N N C V U L P C N Y A Y
Q U Z H N B L O A O G J Q R C J T V T K
S M X G T L N O P N L E X P P Z I I V
Y C Z T E A Q Y R O T P Y L D I V A O R
H M C D D Z H E C N A I G E L L A C N N
```

ABOMINATIONS	BLASPHEMY	FRAUD	PENITENCE
ADAMANT	CALAMITY	HYPOCRITES	PERPLEXED
ALLEGIANCE	CALUMNY	INCREDULOUSLY	PRETENSE
ANARCHY	CONJURED	INDICTMENT	QUAIL
ANONYMITY	CONTEMPLATION	INDIGNANT	QUALM
ANTAGONISTS	CONTENTIOUS	INEPTLY	REPRIEVE
ASCERTAIN	DAFT	INERT	SARCASTICAL
AUDIBLE	DIABOLISM	LECHERY	STATUTES
AVIDLY	ECSTATIC	MANIFEST	TAINTED
BASE	EFFRONTERY	MENACINGLY	TRANSFIXED
BEGUILE	EVADE	PALLOR	
BEMUSED	FACTION	PARTISAN	

The Crucible Vocabulary Word Search 3 Answer Key

ABOMINATIONS	BLASPHEMY	FRAUD	PENITENCE
ADAMANT	CALAMITY	HYPOCRITES	PERPLEXED
ALLEGIANCE	CALUMNY	INCREDULOUSLY	PRETENSE
ANARCHY	CONJURED	INDICTMENT	QUAIL
ANONYMITY	CONTEMPLATION	INDIGNANT	QUALM
ANTAGONISTS	CONTENTIOUS	INEPTLY	REPRIEVE
ASCERTAIN	DAFT	INERT	SARCASTICAL
AUDIBLE	DIABOLISM	LECHERY	STATUTES
AVIDLY	ECSTATIC	MANIFEST	TAINTED
BASE	EFFRONTERY	MENACINGLY	TRANSFIXED
BEGUILE	EVADE	PALLOR	
BEMUSED	FACTION	PARTISAN	

The Crucible Vocabulary Word Search 4

```
P C O N T E M P T U O U S Y R E H C E L
R A P E R P L E X E D Y W T S M H J Y W
O V R N V Z L X B X N L C N A T C H H V
D I A T Y B G W Q M T A E A Q I S V N V
I D J N I R J X U N E T N F L N N O M R
G L Y D T S J L A N E C X A O A I T G H
I Y U K N A A N S R N P S I R T M Z E J
O A R M T C G N P P T G T T C C H I F D
U G N X Z I B O P E Q A H A A Z H W T R
S Q N B D P S D N N N Y F W V T W Y S Y
R N O N E W S U O I T N E C I L I Z T R
E J I D X G P F M T S D T I D F H C A Y
M W T I I B U O C E K T N N J B Y M T X
O A A A F H B I T N G C S E Q R A I U D
R D N B S A X N L C R Y Z R E L M S T L
S A M O N I A T R E C S A T L Y T T E F
E M E L A R W L D X H V N E N Z S C S S
L A D I R X C U C E F O G O K E N D S K
E N N S T G L N V F R I N T F E L X I D
S T O M E O Q E W F A A N I D I R N E R
S F C D U K I W F N U N N I A B E S O M
L S A S T R Z E C H D A V U F P U L L R
Y V L F P J W E Y V M O Q Z T M L A Z C
E Y M E H P S A L B R N L L E A U D R K
D E R U J N O C P P L B Y B P Q G S C H
```

ABOMINATIONS	BLASPHEMY	FRAUD	PRETENSE
ADAMANT	CALAMITY	INCREDULOUSLY	PRODIGIOUS
ALLEGIANCE	CALUMNY	INDIGNANT	PROVIDENCE
ANARCHY	CONDEMNATION	INEPTLY	QUAIL
ANONYMITY	CONJURED	INERT	QUALM
ANTAGONISTS	CONTEMPTUOUS	LECHERY	REMORSELESSLY
ASCERTAIN	DAFT	LICENTIOUS	REPRIEVE
AUDIBLE	DIABOLISM	MANIFEST	STATUTES
AVIDLY	ECSTATIC	PALLOR	TAINTED
BASE	EFFRONTERY	PARTISAN	TRANSFIXED
BEGUILE	EVADE	PENITENCE	
BEMUSED	FACTION	PERPLEXED	

The Crucible Vocabulary Word Search 4 Answer Key

ABOMINATIONS	BLASPHEMY	FRAUD	PRETENSE
ADAMANT	CALAMITY	INCREDULOUSLY	PRODIGIOUS
ALLEGIANCE	CALUMNY	INDIGNANT	PROVIDENCE
ANARCHY	CONDEMNATION	INEPTLY	QUAIL
ANONYMITY	CONJURED	INERT	QUALM
ANTAGONISTS	CONTEMPTUOUS	LECHERY	REMORSELESSLY
ASCERTAIN	DAFT	LICENTIOUS	REPRIEVE
AUDIBLE	DIABOLISM	MANIFEST	STATUTES
AVIDLY	ECSTATIC	PALLOR	TAINTED
BASE	EFFRONTERY	PARTISAN	TRANSFIXED
BEGUILE	EVADE	PENITENCE	
BEMUSED	FACTION	PERPLEXED	

The Crucible Vocabulary Crossword 1

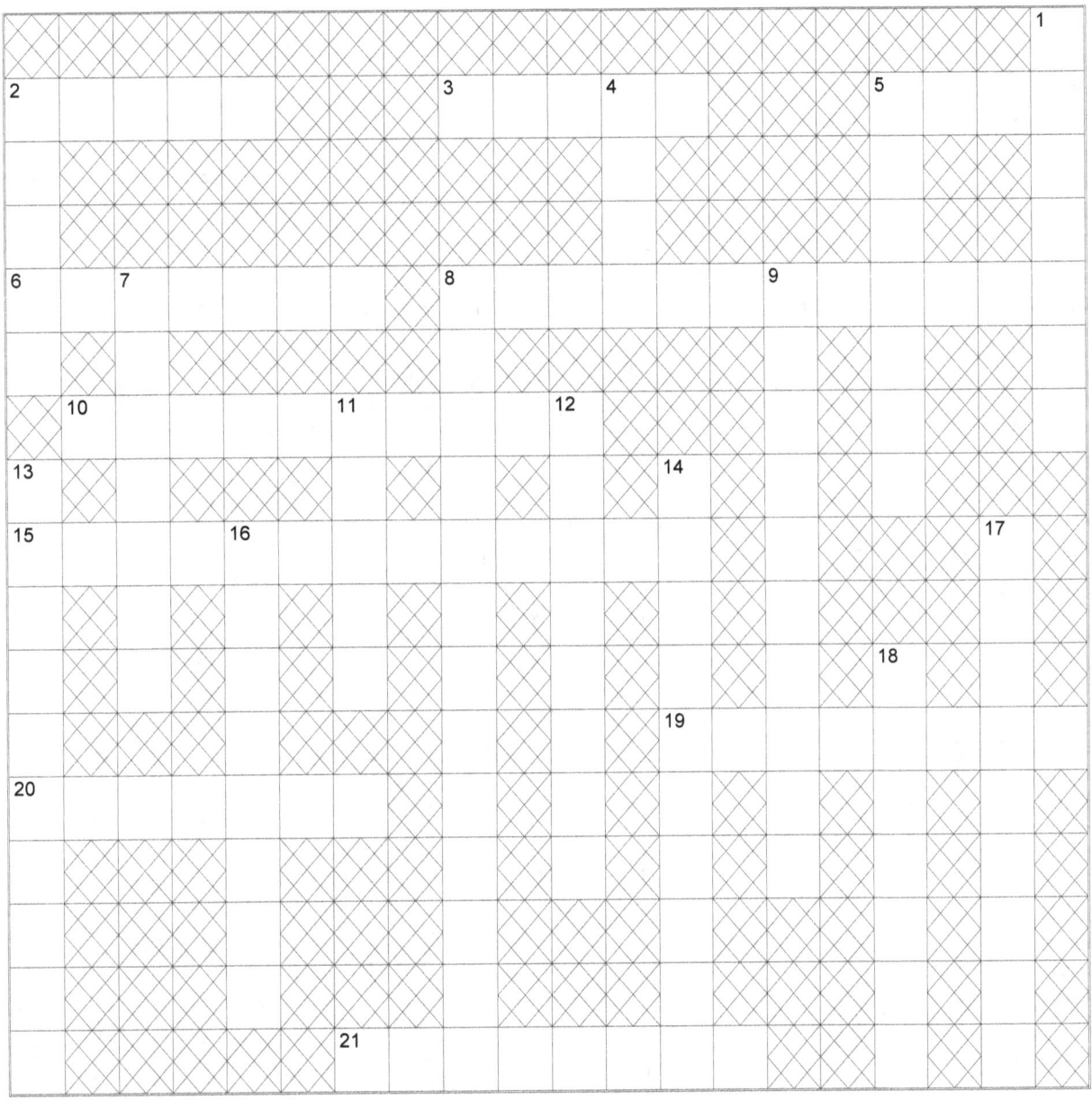

Across
2. To lose courage; decline; fail; give way
3. Escape or avoid by cleverness or deceit
5. Having low moral standards; contemptible; inferior
6. Promiscuity
8. Scornful; distainful
10. Loyalty
15. Mercilessly; having no pity or compassion
19. Summoned by oath or spell
20. Small group of people, usually contentious, within a larger group
21. Something apparent to the sight or understanding

Down
1. Confused
2. Sensation of misgiving or uneasiness
4. Crazy; foolish; stupid
5. Delude; cheat; divert
7. False statement maliciously or knowingly made to injure someone
8. Thoughtful observation or meditation
9. Work of divine direction
11. Unable to move or act
12. In a state of exalted delight
13. Rendered motionless with terror, amazement or awe
14. People who say they believe one way but in actious show they believe the opposite
16. Postponement of punishment
17. Find out
18. Able to be heard

The Crucible Vocabulary Crossword 1 Answer Key

	1 B
2 QUAIL   3 EVADE   4 D   5 BASE E
U   A   E   M
A   F   G   U
6 LECHERY 8 CONTEMPTUOUS
M   A   O   R   I   E
10 ALLEGIANCE 12 E   O   L   D
13 T U   N T   C   14 H V E
15 REMORSELESSLY I   17 A
A   N   E R   M   T   P   D   S
N   Y   P T   P   A   O   E 18 A C
S   R   L   T 19 CONJURED
20 FACTION   A   I   R   C   D   R
I   E   T   C   I   E   I   T
X   V   I   T   B   A
E   E   O   E   L   I
D   21 MANIFEST   E   N

Across
2. To lose courage; decline; fail; give way
3. Escape or avoid by cleverness or deceit
5. Having low moral standards; contemptible; inferior
6. Promiscuity
8. Scornful; distainful
10. Loyalty
15. Mercilessly; having no pity or compassion
19. Summoned by oath or spell
20. Small group of people, usually contentious, within a larger group
21. Something apparent to the sight or understanding

Down
1. Confused
2. Sensation of misgiving or uneasiness
4. Crazy; foolish; stupid
5. Delude; cheat; divert
7. False statement maliciously or knowingly made to injure someone
8. Thoughtful observation or meditation
9. Work of divine direction
11. Unable to move or act
12. In a state of exalted delight
13. Rendered motionless with terror, amazement or awe
14. People who say they believe one way but in actious show they believe the opposite
16. Postponement of punishment
17. Find out
18. Able to be heard

The Crucible Vocabulary Crossword 2

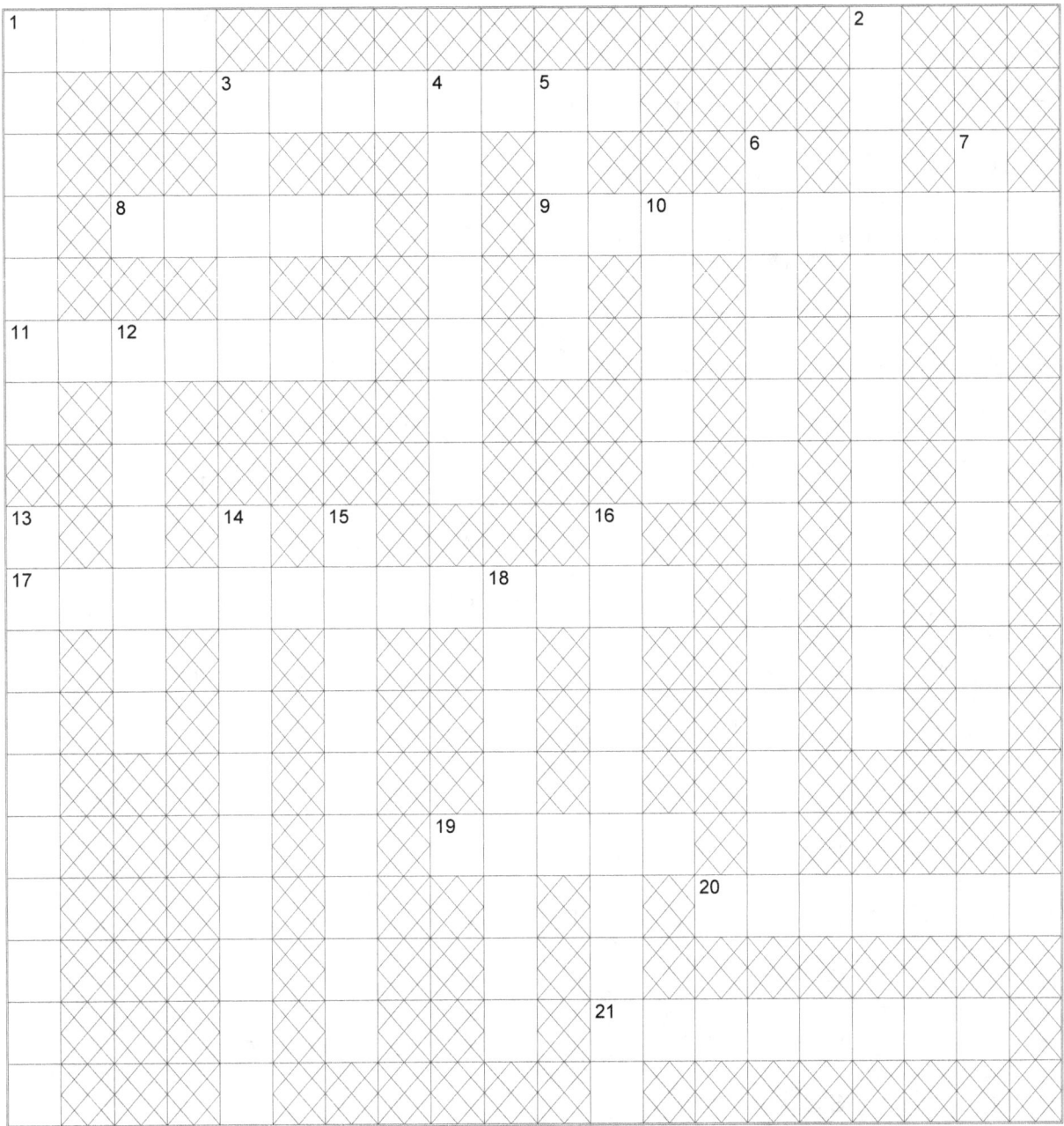

Across
1. Having low moral standards; contemptible; inferior
3. In a state of exalted delight
8. Sensation of misgiving or uneasiness
9. Audacity; insulting boldness
11. Promiscuity
17. Mercilessly; having no pity or compassion
19. To lose courage; decline; fail; give way
20. Awkward
21. Disaster

Down
1. Delude; cheat; divert
2. Scornful; distainful
3. Escape or avoid by cleverness or deceit
4. Political disorder and confusion
5. Unable to move or act
6. Thoughtful observation or meditation
7. Work of divine direction
10. Deliberate deception for unfair or unlawful gain
12. False statement maliciously or knowingly made to injure someone
13. Rendered motionless with terror, amazement or awe
14. Extraordinary; marvelous
15. Performing of penance
16. Loyalty
18. Laws, decrees or edicts

The Crucible Vocabulary Crossword 2 Answer Key

	1												2	
	B	A	S	E									C	
	E				3			4		5			O	
	E				E	C	S	T	A	T	I	C	O	
	G				V			N		N		6	N	7
			8									C		P
	U		Q	U	A	L	M		9		10			
								A	E	F	F	R	O	N	T	E	R	Y
	I			D				R	R	R	N		E		O
11		12												
	L	E	C	H	E	R	Y		C	T	A	T	M		V
	E	A					H			U	E	P		I
		L					Y			D	M	T		D
13			14		15				16				
	T	U		P		P			A		P	U		E
17								18					
	R	E	M	O	R	S	E	L	E	S	S	L	Y	L	O	N
	A	N	O	N		T			L		A	U	C
	N	Y	D	I		A			E		T	S	E
	S		I	T		T			G		I	
	F		G	E		19						
						Q	U	A	I	L	O	
	I		I	N		T			A		20	
											I	N	E	P	T	L	Y
	X		O	C		E			N		
									21	
	E		U	E		S			C	A	L	A	M	I	T	Y
	D		S						E	

Across
1. Having low moral standards; contemptible; inferior
3. In a state of exalted delight
8. Sensation of misgiving or uneasiness
9. Audacity; insulting boldness
11. Promiscuity
17. Mercilessly; having no pity or compassion
19. To lose courage; decline; fail; give way
20. Awkward
21. Disaster

Down
1. Delude; cheat; divert
2. Scornful; distainful
3. Escape or avoid by cleverness or deceit
4. Political disorder and confusion
5. Unable to move or act
6. Thoughtful observation or meditation
7. Work of divine direction
10. Deliberate deception for unfair or unlawful gain
12. False statement maliciously or knowingly made to injure someone
13. Rendered motionless with terror, amazement or awe
14. Extraordinary; marvelous
15. Performing of penance
16. Loyalty
18. Laws, decrees or edicts

The Crucible Vocabulary Crossword 3

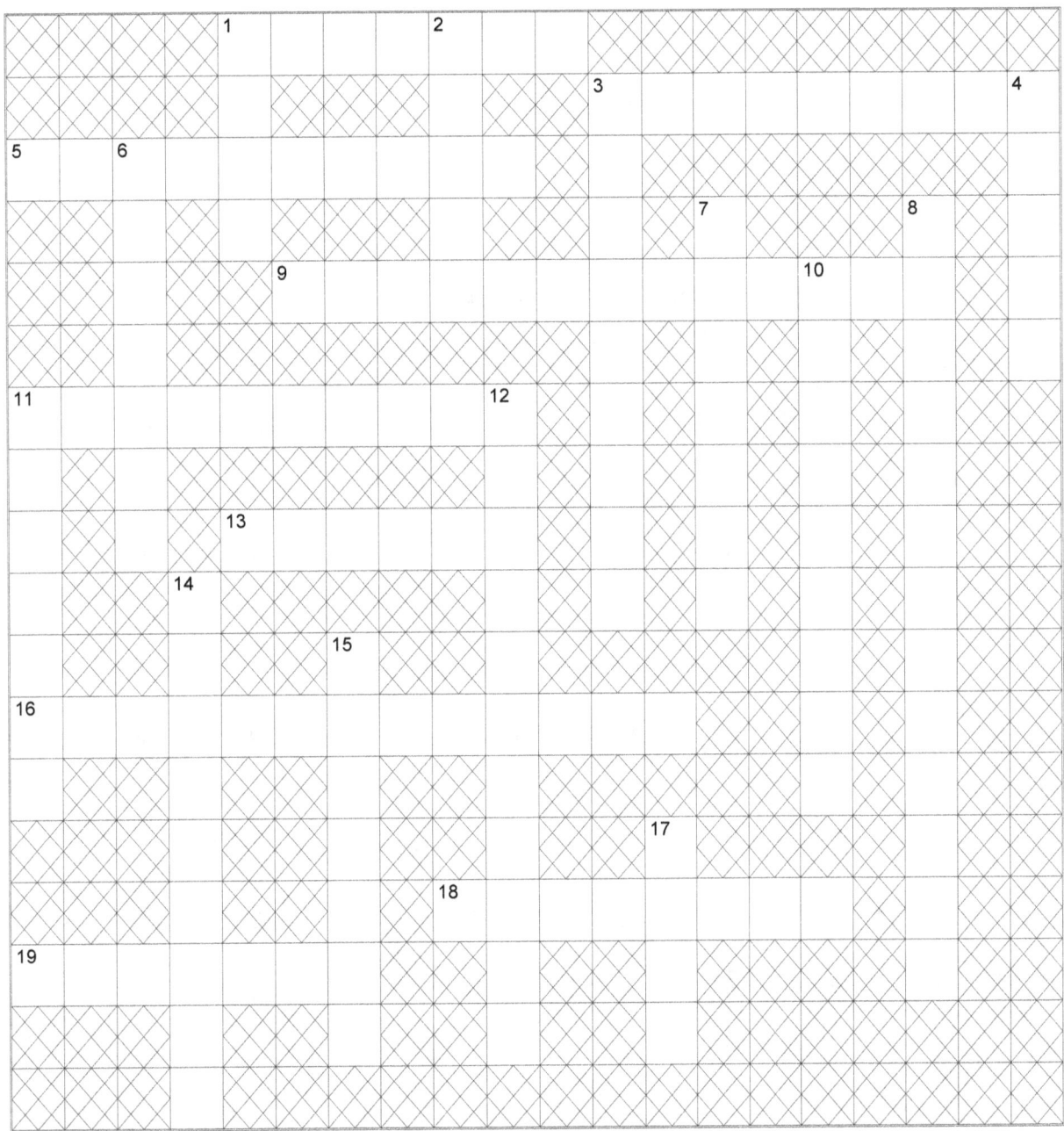

Across
1. Delude; cheat; divert
3. Performing of penance
5. Rendered motionless with terror, amazement or awe
9. Thoughtful observation or meditation
11. Having no regard for accepted rules or standards
13. Extreme paleness
16. Mercilessly; having no pity or compassion
18. In a state of exalted delight
19. Able to be heard

Down
1. Having low moral standards; contemptible; inferior
2. Unable to move or act
3. Bewildered; puzzled; confused
4. Escape or avoid by cleverness or deceit
6. Political disorder and confusion
7. False statement maliciously or knowingly made to injure someone
8. Disbelievingly
10. Filled with an anger aroused by something unjust or unworthy
11. Promiscuity
12. Expressing mocking or contemptuous remarks
14. Secrecy; having unknown or unacknowledged name
15. Confused
17. Crazy; foolish; stupid

The Crucible Vocabulary Crossword 3 Answer Key

Across
1. Delude; cheat; divert
3. Performing of penance
5. Rendered motionless with terror, amazement or awe
9. Thoughtful observation or meditation
11. Having no regard for accepted rules or standards
13. Extreme paleness
16. Mercilessly; having no pity or compassion
18. In a state of exalted delight
19. Able to be heard

Down
1. Having low moral standards; contemptible; inferior
2. Unable to move or act
3. Bewildered; puzzled; confused
4. Escape or avoid by cleverness or deceit
6. Political disorder and confusion
7. False statement maliciously or knowingly made to injure someone
8. Disbelievingly
10. Filled with an anger aroused by something unjust or unworthy
11. Promiscuity
12. Expressing mocking or contemptuous remarks
14. Secrecy; having unknown or unacknowledged name
15. Confused
17. Crazy; foolish; stupid

The Crucible Vocabulary Crossword 4

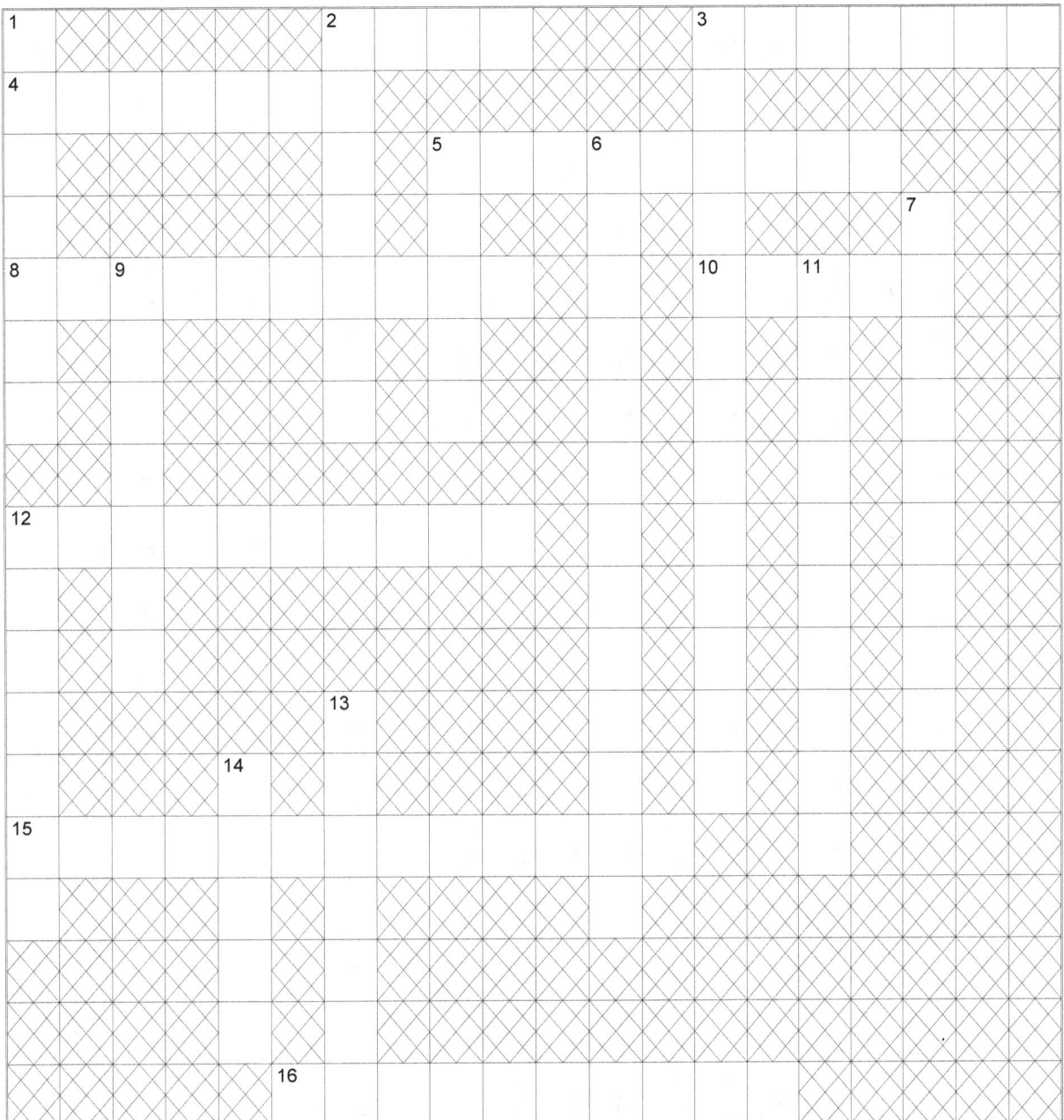

Across
2. Having low moral standards; contemptible; inferior
3. False statement maliciously or knowingly made to injure someone
4. Able to be heard
5. Filled with an anger aroused by something unjust or unworthy
8. Rendered motionless with terror, amazement or awe
10. Escape or avoid by cleverness or deceit
12. Having no regard for accepted rules or standards
15. Mercilessly; having no pity or compassion
16. People who say they believe one way but in actious show they believe the opposite

Down
1. Having a moral defect; infected
2. Delude; cheat; divert
3. Thoughtful observation or meditation
5. Unable to move or act
6. Disbelievingly
7. Performing of penance
9. Political disorder and confusion
11. Loyalty
12. Promiscuity
13. Awkward
14. Deliberate deception for unfair or unlawful gain

The Crucible Vocabulary Crossword 4 Answer Key

Across
2. Having low moral standards; contemptible; inferior
3. False statement maliciously or knowingly made to injure someone
4. Able to be heard
5. Filled with an anger aroused by something unjust or unworthy
8. Rendered motionless with terror, amazement or awe
10. Escape or avoid by cleverness or deceit
12. Having no regard for accepted rules or standards
15. Mercilessly; having no pity or compassion
16. People who say they believe one way but in actious show they believe the opposite

Down
1. Having a moral defect; infected
2. Delude; cheat; divert
3. Thoughtful observation or meditation
5. Unable to move or act
6. Disbelievingly
7. Performing of penance
9. Political disorder and confusion
11. Loyalty
12. Promiscuity
13. Awkward
14. Deliberate deception for unfair or unlawful gain

Answers:

Across: 2. BASE, 3. CALUMNY, 4. AUDIBLE, 5. INDIGNANT, 8. TRANSFIXED, 10. EVADE, 12. LICENTIOUS, 15. REMORSELESSLY, 16. HYPOCRITES

Down: 1. TAINTED, 2. BEGUILE, 3. CONTEMPLATION, 5. INERT, 6. INCREDULOUSLY, 7. PENITENCE, 9. ANARCHY, 11. ALLEGIANCE, 12. LECHERY, 13. INEPT, 14. FRAUD

The Crucible Vocabulary Juggle Letters 1

1. ONPAIOITTPRI = 1. _____
   Appeasement

2. PTCANOTONIMEL = 2. _____
   Thoughtful observation or meditation

3. MBISAODLI = 3. _____
   Witchcraft; sorcery

4. NCDNOEINAMTO = 4. _____
   Severe reproof; strong censure

5. UAQLM = 5. _____
   Sensation of misgiving or uneasiness

6. OMINBSINOATA = 6. _____
   Things that elicit great dislike or abhorrence

7. DEPXEERLP = 7. _____
   Bewildered; puzzled; confused

8. SNETFAMI = 8. _____
   Something apparent to the sight or understanding

9. DITNGNINA = 9. _____
   Filled with an anger aroused by something unjust or unworthy

10. NESTEERP =10. _____
    The act of pretending

11. PILETYN =11. _____
    Awkward

12. AUESTTTS =12. _____
    Laws, decrees or edicts

13. ACYMLUN =13. _____
    False statement maliciously or knowingly made to injure someone

14. MELSBAYHP =14. _____
    An irreverent or impious act or utterance

15. OFEYRRFTEN =15. _____
    Audacity; insulting boldness

The Crucible Vocabulary Juggle Letters 1 Answer Key

1. ONPAIOITTPRI = 1. PROPITIATION
   Appeasement

2. PTCANOTONIMEL = 2. CONTEMPLATION
   Thoughtful observation or meditation

3. MBISAODLI = 3. DIABOLISM
   Witchcraft; sorcery

4. NCDNOEINAMTO = 4. CONDEMNATION
   Severe reproof; strong censure

5. UAQLM = 5. QUALM
   Sensation of misgiving or uneasiness

6. OMINBSINOATA = 6. ABOMINATIONS
   Things that elicit great dislike or abhorrence

7. DEPXEERLP = 7. PERPLEXED
   Bewildered; puzzled; confused

8. SNETFAMI = 8. MANIFEST
   Something apparent to the sight or understanding

9. DITNGNINA = 9. INDIGNANT
   Filled with an anger aroused by something unjust or unworthy

10. NESTEERP =10. PRETENSE
    The act of pretending

11. PILETYN =11. INEPTLY
    Awkward

12. AUESTTTS =12. STATUTES
    Laws, decrees or edicts

13. ACYMLUN =13. CALUMNY
    False statement maliciously or knowingly made to injure someone

14. MELSBAYHP =14. BLASPHEMY
    An irreverent or impious act or utterance

15. OFEYRRFTEN =15. EFFRONTERY
    Audacity; insulting boldness

The Crucible Vocabulary Juggle Letters 2

1. IRIDGOOPUS = 1. _____
   Extraordinary; marvelous

2. DIETNCNMTI = 2. _____
   Statement of criminal charges

3. YILCEAMNGN = 3. _____
   Threateningly

4. MTUSEOPUOTNC = 4. _____
   Scornful; distainful

5. ISTATECC = 5. _____
   In a state of exalted delight

6. EVADE = 6. _____
   Escape or avoid by cleverness or deceit

7. IFETANSM = 7. _____
   Something apparent to the sight or understanding

8. IEVEREPR = 8. _____
   Postponement of punishment

9. TEFRONYFRE = 9. _____
   Audacity; insulting boldness

10. QLAUM = 10. _____
    Sensation of misgiving or uneasiness

11. TIOIPTOIPRAN = 11. _____
    Appeasement

12. EOIANNDNOCMT = 12. _____
    Severe reproof; strong censure

13. ACYAITLM = 13. _____
    Disaster

14. NTIADET = 14. _____
    Having a moral defect; infected

15. TNDAAAM = 15. _____
    Firm in purpose or opinion; unyielding

The Crucible Vocabulary Juggle Letters 2 Answer Key

1. IRIDGOOPUS   = 1. PRODIGIOUS
                           Extraordinary; marvelous

2. DIETNCNMTI   = 2. INDICTMENT
                           Statement of criminal charges

3. YILCEAMNGN   = 3. MENACINGLY
                           Threateningly

4. MTUSEOPUOTNC   = 4. CONTEMPTUOUS
                           Scornful; distainful

5. ISTATECC   = 5. ECSTATIC
                           In a state of exalted delight

6. EVADE   = 6. EVADE
                           Escape or avoid by cleverness or deceit

7. IFETANSM   = 7. MANIFEST
                           Something apparent to the sight or understanding

8. IEVEREPR   = 8. REPRIEVE
                           Postponement of punishment

9. TEFRONYFRE   = 9. EFFRONTERY
                           Audacity; insulting boldness

10. QLAUM   =10. QUALM
                           Sensation of misgiving or uneasiness

11. TIOIPTOIPRAN   =11. PROPITIATION
                           Appeasement

12. EOIANNDNOCMT   =12. CONDEMNATION
                           Severe reproof; strong censure

13. ACYAITLM   =13. CALAMITY
                           Disaster

14. NTIADET   =14. TAINTED
                           Having a moral defect; infected

15. TNDAAAM   =15. ADAMANT
                           Firm in purpose or opinion; unyielding

The Crucible Vocabulary Juggle Letters 3

1. AHPLEBSMY = 1. _____
   An irreverent or impious act or utterance

2. LIDAUEB = 2. _____
   Able to be heard

3. ABIOLDMIS = 3. _____
   Witchcraft; sorcery

4. RPPXEEDLE = 4. _____
   Bewildered; puzzled; confused

5. HCEELRY = 5. _____
   Promiscuity

6. NIETNTCMID = 6. _____
   Statement of criminal charges

7. ANNMEIODCNTO = 7. _____
   Severe reproof; strong censure

8. EEDVA = 8. _____
   Escape or avoid by cleverness or deceit

9. TSENPEER = 9. _____
   The act of pretending

10. OCDVEENRPI = 10. _____
    Work of divine direction

11. LLSYUNOIDRECU = 11. _____
    Disbelievingly

12. SABE = 12. _____
    Having low moral standards; contemptible; inferior

13. ARFDU = 13. _____
    Deliberate deception for unfair or unlawful gain

14. HYAACNR = 14. _____
    Political disorder and confusion

15. RPATNIAS = 15. _____
    Militant supporter of a party, cause, faction or idea

The Crucible Vocabulary Juggle Letters 3 Answer Key

1. AHPLEBSMY = 1. BLASPHEMY
   An irreverent or impious act or utterance

2. LIDAUEB = 2. AUDIBLE
   Able to be heard

3. ABIOLDMIS = 3. DIABOLISM
   Witchcraft; sorcery

4. RPPXEEDLE = 4. PERPLEXED
   Bewildered; puzzled; confused

5. HCEELRY = 5. LECHERY
   Promiscuity

6. NIETNTCMID = 6. INDICTMENT
   Statement of criminal charges

7. ANNMEIODCNTO = 7. CONDEMNATION
   Severe reproof; strong censure

8. EEDVA = 8. EVADE
   Escape or avoid by cleverness or deceit

9. TSENPEER = 9. PRETENSE
   The act of pretending

10. OCDVEENRPI = 10. PROVIDENCE
    Work of divine direction

11. LLSYUNOIDRECU = 11. INCREDULOUSLY
    Disbelievingly

12. SABE = 12. BASE
    Having low moral standards; contemptible; inferior

13. ARFDU = 13. FRAUD
    Deliberate deception for unfair or unlawful gain

14. HYAACNR = 14. ANARCHY
    Political disorder and confusion

15. RPATNIAS = 15. PARTISAN
    Militant supporter of a party, cause, faction or idea

The Crucible Vocabulary Juggle Letters 4

1. LOARLP = 1. _____
   Extreme paleness

2. TYHSCRIEPO = 2. _____
   People who say they believe one way but in actious show they believe the opposite

3. OIFTNAC = 3. _____
   Small group of people, usually contentious, within a larger group

4. CNDIEITTMN = 4. _____
   Statement of criminal charges

5. TMNYIAONY = 5. _____
   Secrecy; having unknown or unacknowledged name

6. IANTOMINOSAB = 6. _____
   Things that elicit great dislike or abhorrence

7. MQLAU = 7. _____
   Sensation of misgiving or uneasiness

8. URIODOIGSP = 8. _____
   Extraordinary; marvelous

9. ICTAYLMA = 9. _____
   Disaster

10. ACENNGIMYL = 10. _____
    Threateningly

11. PRRVEIEE = 11. _____
    Postponement of punishment

12. OOAIMNECNTDN = 12. _____
    Severe reproof; strong censure

13. UIALQ = 13. _____
    To lose courage; decline; fail; give way

14. IEULDBA = 14. _____
    Able to be heard

15. ESAB = 15. _____
    Having low moral standards; contemptible; inferior

The Crucible Vocabulary Juggle Letters 4 Answer Key

1. LOARLP = 1. PALLOR
   Extreme paleness

2. TYHSCRIEPO = 2. HYPOCRITES
   People who say they believe one way but in actious show they believe the opposite

3. OIFTNAC = 3. FACTION
   Small group of people, usually contentious, within a larger group

4. CNDIEITTMN = 4. INDICTMENT
   Statement of criminal charges

5. TMNYIAONY = 5. ANONYMITY
   Secrecy; having unknown or unacknowledged name

6. IANTOMINOSAB = 6. ABOMINATIONS
   Things that elicit great dislike or abhorrence

7. MQLAU = 7. QUALM
   Sensation of misgiving or uneasiness

8. URIODOIGSP = 8. PRODIGIOUS
   Extraordinary; marvelous

9. ICTAYLMA = 9. CALAMITY
   Disaster

10. ACENNGIMYL = 10. MENACINGLY
    Threateningly

11. PRRVEIEE = 11. REPRIEVE
    Postponement of punishment

12. OOAIMNECNTDN = 12. CONDEMNATION
    Severe reproof; strong censure

13. UIALQ = 13. QUAIL
    To lose courage; decline; fail; give way

14. IEULDBA = 14. AUDIBLE
    Able to be heard

15. ESAB = 15. BASE
    Having low moral standards; contemptible; inferior

ABOMINATIONS	Things that elicit great dislike or abhorrence
ADAMANT	Firm in purpose or opinion; unyielding
ALLEGIANCE	Loyalty
ANARCHY	Political disorder and confusion
ANONYMITY	Secrecy; having unknown or unacknowledged name
ANTAGONISTS	Adversaries; opponents

ASCERTAIN	Find out
AUDIBLE	Able to be heard
AVIDLY	Enthusiastically
BASE	Having low moral standards; contemptible; inferior
BEGUILE	Delude; cheat; divert
BEMUSED	Confused

BLASPHEMY	An irreverent or impious act or utterance
CALAMITY	Disaster
CALUMNY	False statement maliciously or knowingly made to injure someone
CONDEMNATION	Severe reproof; strong censure
CONJURED	Summoned by oath or spell
CONTEMPLATION	Thoughtful observation or meditation

CONTEMPTUOUS	Scornful; distainful
CONTENTIOUS	Quarrelsome
DAFT	Crazy; foolish; stupid
DIABOLISM	Witchcraft; sorcery
ECSTATIC	In a state of exalted delight
EFFRONTERY	Audacity; insulting boldness

EVADE	Escape or avoid by cleverness or deceit
FACTION	Small group of people, usually contentious, within a larger group
FRAUD	Deliberate deception for unfair or unlawful gain
HYPOCRITES	People who say they believe one way but in actious show they believe the opposite
INCREDULOUSLY	Disbelievingly
INDICTMENT	Statement of criminal charges

INDIGNANT	Filled with an anger aroused by something unjust or unworthy
INEPTLY	Awkward
INERT	Unable to move or act
LECHERY	Promiscuity
LICENTIOUS	Having no regard for accepted rules or standards
MANIFEST	Something apparent to the sight or understanding

MENACINGLY	Threateningly
PALLOR	Extreme paleness
PARTISAN	Militant supporter of a party, cause, faction or idea
PENITENCE	Performing of penance
PERPLEXED	Bewildered; puzzled; confused
PRETENSE	The act of pretending

PRODIGIOUS	Extraordinary; marvelous
PROPITIATION	Appeasement
PROVIDENCE	Work of divine direction
QUAIL	To lose courage; decline; fail; give way
QUALM	Sensation of misgiving or uneasiness
REMORSELESSLY	Mercilessly; having no pity or compassion

REPRIEVE	Postponement of punishment
SARCASTICAL	Expressing mocking or contemptuous remarks
STATUTES	Laws, decrees or edicts
TAINTED	Having a moral defect; infected
TRANSFIXED	Rendered motionless with terror, amazement or awe

The Crucible Vocabulary

FRAUD	PALLOR	AVIDLY	EVADE	ADAMANT
FACTION	ABOMINATIONS	REMORSELESSLY	CONTEMPLATION	DIABOLISM
INERT	CALAMITY	FREE SPACE	INEPTLY	HYPOCRITES
PRODIGIOUS	EFFRONTERY	INDIGNANT	STATUTES	QUAIL
BLASPHEMY	PENITENCE	CONTEMPTUOUS	BEGUILE	ANONYMITY

The Crucible Vocabulary

BEMUSED	CONJURED	PRETENSE	LICENTIOUS	INCREDULOUSLY
ASCERTAIN	BASE	PROVIDENCE	PARTISAN	PERPLEXED
SARCASTICAL	CONDEMNATION	FREE SPACE	TRANSFIXED	TAINTED
CALUMNY	CONTENTIOUS	INDICTMENT	ANTAGONISTS	REPRIEVE
ECSTATIC	DAFT	AUDIBLE	ALLEGIANCE	ANARCHY

The Crucible Vocabulary

PERPLEXED	MENACINGLY	STATUTES	BLASPHEMY	QUALM
DIABOLISM	TAINTED	LICENTIOUS	ADAMANT	ALLEGIANCE
ABOMINATIONS	CALUMNY	FREE SPACE	CONTENTIOUS	ANARCHY
INEPTLY	HYPOCRITES	REPRIEVE	INERT	CALAMITY
DAFT	REMORSELESSLY	INCREDULOUSLY	PRETENSE	SARCASTICAL

The Crucible Vocabulary

BASE	MANIFEST	FACTION	INDICTMENT	ANTAGONISTS
BEMUSED	BEGUILE	CONTEMPLATION	CONJURED	PROPITIATION
AUDIBLE	EFFRONTERY	FREE SPACE	AVIDLY	INDIGNANT
ECSTATIC	PRODIGIOUS	PALLOR	ASCERTAIN	TRANSFIXED
LECHERY	QUAIL	CONTEMPTUOUS	PARTISAN	EVADE

The Crucible Vocabulary

MANIFEST	ALLEGIANCE	MENACINGLY	CALUMNY	PRETENSE
INDICTMENT	TRANSFIXED	BLASPHEMY	ANTAGONISTS	CALAMITY
QUAIL	STATUTES	FREE SPACE	CONTEMPTUOUS	PARTISAN
ANARCHY	CONDEMNATION	FRAUD	CONTEMPLATION	QUALM
HYPOCRITES	LECHERY	DIABOLISM	TAINTED	REMORSELESSLY

The Crucible Vocabulary

ASCERTAIN	PROVIDENCE	PALLOR	BEGUILE	REPRIEVE
BEMUSED	LICENTIOUS	ABOMINATIONS	BASE	SARCASTICAL
ECSTATIC	CONTENTIOUS	FREE SPACE	EVADE	CONJURED
PERPLEXED	AUDIBLE	INERT	INCREDULOUSLY	FACTION
EFFRONTERY	PRODIGIOUS	PROPITIATION	ADAMANT	ANONYMITY

The Crucible Vocabulary

HYPOCRITES	FRAUD	INEPTLY	BASE	DAFT
STATUTES	EFFRONTERY	REPRIEVE	QUAIL	CALUMNY
AVIDLY	FACTION	FREE SPACE	CALAMITY	MENACINGLY
ANTAGONISTS	PRETENSE	ASCERTAIN	AUDIBLE	TAINTED
INDIGNANT	ANARCHY	BLASPHEMY	LECHERY	ANONYMITY

The Crucible Vocabulary

PERPLEXED	SARCASTICAL	BEGUILE	CONJURED	ABOMINATIONS
TRANSFIXED	BEMUSED	CONTEMPLATION	CONTEMPTUOUS	ALLEGIANCE
LICENTIOUS	ADAMANT	FREE SPACE	PRODIGIOUS	CONDEMNATION
PALLOR	INCREDULOUSLY	DIABOLISM	INDICTMENT	ECSTATIC
PROVIDENCE	PROPITIATION	CONTENTIOUS	MANIFEST	REMORSELESSLY

The Crucible Vocabulary

CONTEMPTUOUS	DIABOLISM	REPRIEVE	QUALM	PENITENCE
REMORSELESSLY	CONTENTIOUS	PROVIDENCE	ANTAGONISTS	LICENTIOUS
MANIFEST	CALAMITY	FREE SPACE	AVIDLY	INCREDULOUSLY
AUDIBLE	INDICTMENT	BLASPHEMY	INDIGNANT	FACTION
PRODIGIOUS	PRETENSE	PERPLEXED	STATUTES	ABOMINATIONS

The Crucible Vocabulary

ECSTATIC	EVADE	BASE	CONTEMPLATION	SARCASTICAL
ASCERTAIN	CALUMNY	ANONYMITY	INEPTLY	PROPITIATION
TAINTED	ALLEGIANCE	FREE SPACE	MENACINGLY	ADAMANT
BEMUSED	CONJURED	TRANSFIXED	DAFT	CONDEMNATION
ANARCHY	INERT	BEGUILE	QUAIL	PALLOR

The Crucible Vocabulary

AVIDLY	DAFT	BEGUILE	STATUTES	INCREDULOUSLY
CONTEMPTUOUS	ECSTATIC	FRAUD	EFFRONTERY	AUDIBLE
CONTEMPLATION	BASE	FREE SPACE	INDIGNANT	MENACINGLY
ANTAGONISTS	EVADE	PRETENSE	INERT	INEPTLY
LICENTIOUS	FACTION	ASCERTAIN	TAINTED	ADAMANT

The Crucible Vocabulary

LECHERY	HYPOCRITES	REPRIEVE	INDICTMENT	PRODIGIOUS
CALUMNY	TRANSFIXED	PROPITIATION	REMORSELESSLY	QUAIL
ANARCHY	SARCASTICAL	FREE SPACE	CONDEMNATION	ANONYMITY
PARTISAN	CONJURED	BEMUSED	CALAMITY	PENITENCE
MANIFEST	DIABOLISM	PROVIDENCE	CONTENTIOUS	ALLEGIANCE

The Crucible Vocabulary

BEMUSED	CALAMITY	EVADE	CONDEMNATION	REMORSELESSLY
INDICTMENT	PRETENSE	BEGUILE	CONJURED	REPRIEVE
BLASPHEMY	LECHERY	FREE SPACE	ABOMINATIONS	PALLOR
PROVIDENCE	MANIFEST	ANTAGONISTS	FRAUD	LICENTIOUS
DAFT	TAINTED	INCREDULOUSLY	MENACINGLY	PRODIGIOUS

The Crucible Vocabulary

CONTEMPLATION	INDIGNANT	STATUTES	ECSTATIC	ANONYMITY
CALUMNY	HYPOCRITES	PROPITIATION	ALLEGIANCE	ANARCHY
QUAIL	AVIDLY	FREE SPACE	QUALM	PENITENCE
DIABOLISM	TRANSFIXED	ADAMANT	BASE	INEPTLY
CONTENTIOUS	SARCASTICAL	EFFRONTERY	PERPLEXED	FACTION

The Crucible Vocabulary

QUAIL	CALUMNY	STATUTES	CONDEMNATION	BASE
TRANSFIXED	REPRIEVE	LECHERY	FACTION	ANTAGONISTS
PALLOR	CONTENTIOUS	FREE SPACE	CONTEMPLATION	AUDIBLE
EFFRONTERY	PROPITIATION	INDIGNANT	ALLEGIANCE	PARTISAN
PRODIGIOUS	DIABOLISM	LICENTIOUS	HYPOCRITES	CONJURED

The Crucible Vocabulary

ADAMANT	SARCASTICAL	QUALM	INCREDULOUSLY	ECSTATIC
BEGUILE	CONTEMPTUOUS	CALAMITY	ASCERTAIN	FRAUD
INDICTMENT	PROVIDENCE	FREE SPACE	INEPTLY	PENITENCE
ABOMINATIONS	BLASPHEMY	ANARCHY	BEMUSED	ANONYMITY
DAFT	TAINTED	PRETENSE	EVADE	PERPLEXED

The Crucible Vocabulary

MANIFEST	MENACINGLY	INDIGNANT	QUALM	BEMUSED
BLASPHEMY	INDICTMENT	BASE	STATUTES	CALAMITY
FACTION	EFFRONTERY	FREE SPACE	PRODIGIOUS	ECSTATIC
REMORSELESSLY	DAFT	LECHERY	AVIDLY	SARCASTICAL
TAINTED	ANTAGONISTS	CONTEMPTUOUS	ADAMANT	FRAUD

The Crucible Vocabulary

PRETENSE	INEPTLY	ASCERTAIN	HYPOCRITES	INCREDULOUSLY
AUDIBLE	CONTENTIOUS	CALUMNY	ANONYMITY	CONTEMPLATION
DIABOLISM	PERPLEXED	FREE SPACE	ALLEGIANCE	PROPITIATION
CONJURED	CONDEMNATION	REPRIEVE	TRANSFIXED	PALLOR
BEGUILE	PROVIDENCE	QUAIL	PENITENCE	EVADE

The Crucible Vocabulary

INDICTMENT	ANTAGONISTS	CALUMNY	AUDIBLE	BEMUSED
ECSTATIC	EVADE	REPRIEVE	CALAMITY	BEGUILE
FRAUD	CONTEMPLATION	FREE SPACE	ANONYMITY	QUAIL
PROVIDENCE	LICENTIOUS	CONTEMPTUOUS	ASCERTAIN	INERT
PRODIGIOUS	STATUTES	ANARCHY	BLASPHEMY	REMORSELESSLY

The Crucible Vocabulary

INCREDULOUSLY	PRETENSE	BASE	ADAMANT	MANIFEST
INEPTLY	PERPLEXED	PARTISAN	CONTENTIOUS	MENACINGLY
CONDEMNATION	TAINTED	FREE SPACE	SARCASTICAL	PENITENCE
INDIGNANT	ABOMINATIONS	PALLOR	DAFT	LECHERY
FACTION	CONJURED	EFFRONTERY	QUALM	AVIDLY

The Crucible Vocabulary

PARTISAN	QUALM	INERT	PENITENCE	INDIGNANT
ECSTATIC	EFFRONTERY	INDICTMENT	CONTENTIOUS	ANONYMITY
PERPLEXED	INCREDULOUSLY	FREE SPACE	BLASPHEMY	STATUTES
ANTAGONISTS	BASE	CALAMITY	ANARCHY	FACTION
QUAIL	REPRIEVE	SARCASTICAL	DAFT	PALLOR

The Crucible Vocabulary

AVIDLY	BEMUSED	EVADE	INEPTLY	LICENTIOUS
ASCERTAIN	TAINTED	ALLEGIANCE	BEGUILE	CONDEMNATION
PROVIDENCE	TRANSFIXED	FREE SPACE	PRETENSE	DIABOLISM
REMORSELESSLY	CONTEMPTUOUS	ABOMINATIONS	CALUMNY	CONTEMPLATION
CONJURED	PRODIGIOUS	FRAUD	HYPOCRITES	LECHERY

The Crucible Vocabulary

PALLOR	ANARCHY	INEPTLY	PERPLEXED	QUAIL
DIABOLISM	CONTEMPLATION	REPRIEVE	QUALM	SARCASTICAL
PENITENCE	ASCERTAIN	FREE SPACE	INERT	ALLEGIANCE
STATUTES	INCREDULOUSLY	ANTAGONISTS	LICENTIOUS	CONDEMNATION
EFFRONTERY	PROVIDENCE	CONJURED	CALUMNY	TAINTED

The Crucible Vocabulary

DAFT	MENACINGLY	FACTION	TRANSFIXED	PRETENSE
CALAMITY	PARTISAN	PRODIGIOUS	FRAUD	BLASPHEMY
ANONYMITY	HYPOCRITES	FREE SPACE	LECHERY	CONTENTIOUS
INDIGNANT	ECSTATIC	BEGUILE	BASE	BEMUSED
ADAMANT	MANIFEST	PROPITIATION	AUDIBLE	CONTEMPTUOUS

The Crucible Vocabulary

DAFT	FRAUD	PROPITIATION	CONTENTIOUS	INDIGNANT
REPRIEVE	PARTISAN	PRETENSE	ASCERTAIN	INCREDULOUSLY
EVADE	PALLOR	FREE SPACE	BEMUSED	PRODIGIOUS
ANTAGONISTS	BASE	AUDIBLE	QUAIL	CONTEMPLATION
BLASPHEMY	SARCASTICAL	ANONYMITY	ADAMANT	TRANSFIXED

The Crucible Vocabulary

PENITENCE	MANIFEST	ALLEGIANCE	CONJURED	AVIDLY
ECSTATIC	LECHERY	PROVIDENCE	CONTEMPTUOUS	HYPOCRITES
QUALM	CALAMITY	FREE SPACE	ANARCHY	FACTION
CONDEMNATION	TAINTED	MENACINGLY	ABOMINATIONS	INDICTMENT
LICENTIOUS	BEGUILE	PERPLEXED	EFFRONTERY	STATUTES

The Crucible Vocabulary

ANONYMITY	DAFT	BLASPHEMY	PALLOR	MENACINGLY
BASE	STATUTES	ABOMINATIONS	PROPITIATION	AUDIBLE
PENITENCE	INERT	FREE SPACE	EFFRONTERY	AVIDLY
QUALM	INCREDULOUSLY	CALUMNY	ANTAGONISTS	PARTISAN
FACTION	ANARCHY	QUAIL	DIABOLISM	INEPTLY

The Crucible Vocabulary

PERPLEXED	PROVIDENCE	CONTENTIOUS	LECHERY	PRODIGIOUS
BEGUILE	BEMUSED	ASCERTAIN	ECSTATIC	ALLEGIANCE
INDIGNANT	PRETENSE	FREE SPACE	CONTEMPTUOUS	TRANSFIXED
CONDEMNATION	CONTEMPLATION	CONJURED	FRAUD	SARCASTICAL
HYPOCRITES	TAINTED	CALAMITY	MANIFEST	EVADE

The Crucible Vocabulary

PERPLEXED	ECSTATIC	DAFT	ANONYMITY	LECHERY
TAINTED	PRETENSE	AVIDLY	MENACINGLY	REMORSELESSLY
EVADE	FRAUD	FREE SPACE	ANTAGONISTS	EFFRONTERY
BLASPHEMY	INEPTLY	QUAIL	REPRIEVE	BASE
STATUTES	CALAMITY	INERT	TRANSFIXED	SARCASTICAL

The Crucible Vocabulary

ASCERTAIN	CONDEMNATION	PENITENCE	HYPOCRITES	LICENTIOUS
FACTION	CONTEMPLATION	CONJURED	PROPITIATION	CONTENTIOUS
PALLOR	INCREDULOUSLY	FREE SPACE	AUDIBLE	BEGUILE
PRODIGIOUS	INDIGNANT	QUALM	ANARCHY	ALLEGIANCE
ABOMINATIONS	CONTEMPTUOUS	PROVIDENCE	PARTISAN	MANIFEST

The Crucible Vocabulary

REPRIEVE	CONTENTIOUS	TRANSFIXED	BLASPHEMY	ALLEGIANCE
CALUMNY	CONTEMPLATION	BEMUSED	FACTION	REMORSELESSLY
LICENTIOUS	FRAUD	FREE SPACE	PALLOR	HYPOCRITES
ASCERTAIN	DAFT	PROPITIATION	TAINTED	PROVIDENCE
INEPTLY	PARTISAN	CONDEMNATION	INCREDULOUSLY	MANIFEST

The Crucible Vocabulary

CALAMITY	ABOMINATIONS	BEGUILE	DIABOLISM	BASE
QUALM	SARCASTICAL	EVADE	STATUTES	AUDIBLE
LECHERY	ANARCHY	FREE SPACE	QUAIL	CONTEMPTUOUS
ECSTATIC	ANTAGONISTS	ANONYMITY	EFFRONTERY	ADAMANT
PRODIGIOUS	CONJURED	PRETENSE	PERPLEXED	MENACINGLY